*The*

# FAIRMONT

# EMPRESS

# The FAIRMONT EMPRESS

## The First Hundred Years

TERRY REKSTEN

Douglas & McIntyre

VANCOUVER/TORONTO

Douglas & McIntyre Ltd.
2323 Quebec Street, Suite 201
Vancouver, British Columbia  V5T 4S7
www.douglas-mcintyre.com

*Library and Archives Canada Cataloguing in Publication*
Reksten, Terry, 1942–
The Fairmont Empress : the first hundred years / Terry Reksten.

Previously published under title: The Empress Hotel.
Includes bibliographical references and index.

ISBN 978-1-55365-192-5

1.Empress Hotel—History.  2.Victoria (B.C.)—History.  1.Title.
TX941.E5R44 2008    647.9409711'28    C2007-906250-4

Editing by Saeko Usukawa
Design by DesignGeist
Front cover image © Tim Thompson/CORBIS
Printed and bound in Canada by Friesens
Printed on acid-free paper

We gratefully acknowledge the financial support of the Canada Council for the Arts, the British Columbia Arts Council, the Province of British Columbia through the Book Publishing Tax Credit, and the Government of Canada through the Book Publishing Industry Development Program (BPIDP) for our publishing activities.

*Frontispiece photo,*

B.C. ARCHIVES F-02125

# CONTENTS

# ACKNOWLEDGEMENTS

The idea for this book came from CP Hotels Regional Vice President John Williams who, because he was looking for an objective history, allowed me to work unimpeded. Both he and CP Hotels President Robert DeMone spoke frankly about the Empress's past and future. Paul Jeffery provided information about the hotel's recent past. Nancy Battet guided the way through the CP Archives. Deborah Lloyd Forrest provided insights into the 1989 restoration. And Deirdre Campbell helped in a variety of ways.

Former members of the Empress staff, Louis Finamore, Ken Woodward, Barney Lane, Lloyd Strickland, Eric Penty, Ben Swindell, Jack Ellett, Adrien Regimbal, Peter Shippen, Sylvia Kelly, Pearl Pilip, Roland Linder, John Adams, John Steeves, Jim Walton, Ted Griffin, Bessie Peppers, Bill Reynolds and Marguerite West shared their reminiscences and, in many cases, also allowed me to borrow photographs and other hotel memorabilia.

Also sharing photographs and memories and providing me with enough stories to fill another book were Mabel Sorensen, Shannon Bell, Dolores Stevens, Don Hume, Charlene and Bill Rees, Gladys Gilbert, Ken Stofer, Jack Blain, Ken Leeming, Dorothy Hart, Mrs. G. Smith, David Hill, Jim Ryan, Malcolm Anderson, Hugh Stephen, Dr. Pierre D'Estrube, George Mackay, Ross "Bud" Hocking, Ruth Abel, Joy Smith, Flora McGregor, Pat and Diane Zanachelli, Gloria Bergdahl, Margaret Mosley, Barbara Findlay, Bruce Dickey, Virginia McPhee, Mrs. John Travis, Betty McGrath, Joan Crysler, Gerri Elliott, Lois Duggan, Pat Salmon, Jack Rhodes, Maureen Duffus, Drew Waveryn, Mrs. Charles E. Topp, Eric Charman, Mrs. Radtke, Don Corner, Fred McLeod, Marion Fullerton, Violet Gee and Phyllis Senese. (My apologies to anyone I have inadvertently omitted.)

Richard Mackie, Rosemary Crawford and Bruce Lowther were generous with their own research. And I am particularly grateful to Bill McKee and Georgeen Barras who, at one time, had planned to write a history of the Empress and who generously lent me all their research material.

Mike Wyatt drafted copies of original plans and sketches. George Radford allowed me to use his collection of historic post cards. Stuart Stark provided design insights. Fred Hook, Jennifer Lort and Cyril Hume gave me advice about the gardens. Greg Ovstaas helped me understand complicated construction details and also arranged for me to borrow copies of original plans. Nick Bawlf provided details about the conference centre. Bill Rea offered information about the 1989 renovation. John Taylor rephotographed images and ephemera from people's private collections. And Candy Wyatt provided encouragement and filled her traditional role of "spell checker."

Thanks are also due to Patrick Murphy, Jim Gibson and Joe Easingwood, who drew this project to the public's attention, allowing me to contact many more people than I otherwise might.

My family came through, once again. Don endured endless hours of discussion and then proofread the final text. Jane did research at the Glenbow in Calgary; Norah not only read an early version of the manuscript and gave helpful comments but also compiled the index.

My special thanks to Jim Munro for his support of this project. And, finally, to Scott McIntyre and Saeko Usukawa of Douglas & McIntyre for their work on behalf of the book.

TERRY REKSTEN


I was honoured to be asked to continue the work of the late Terry Reksten, bringing this history of the Fairmont Empress into the twenty-first century. My thanks to Terry's husband, Don, who gave his blessing to the project; to Empress manager Roger Soane, for initiating and supporting the addition of a new chapter; to Deirdre Campbell, for her enthusiasm and memories; to Paul Jeffery, for sharing his intimate knowledge of the hotel and always being there when needed; to Mai Lai, for her help and co-ordination; to former manager John Williams; and to Empress staff members Lawrie Harrison, Stig Karlsson, Andrew Leslie, Lennie Lim, Deborah Sleno, Marlene Watson, Soso Wong and many others who provided information and assistance; and to John Adams, Eric Charman and Rick Arora for information provided.

ROSEMARY NEERING

# Part One

# THE CITY
# AND THE CPR

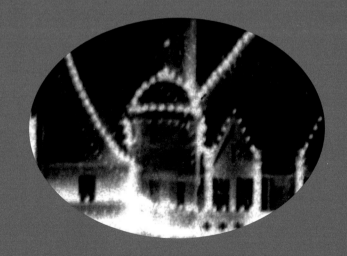

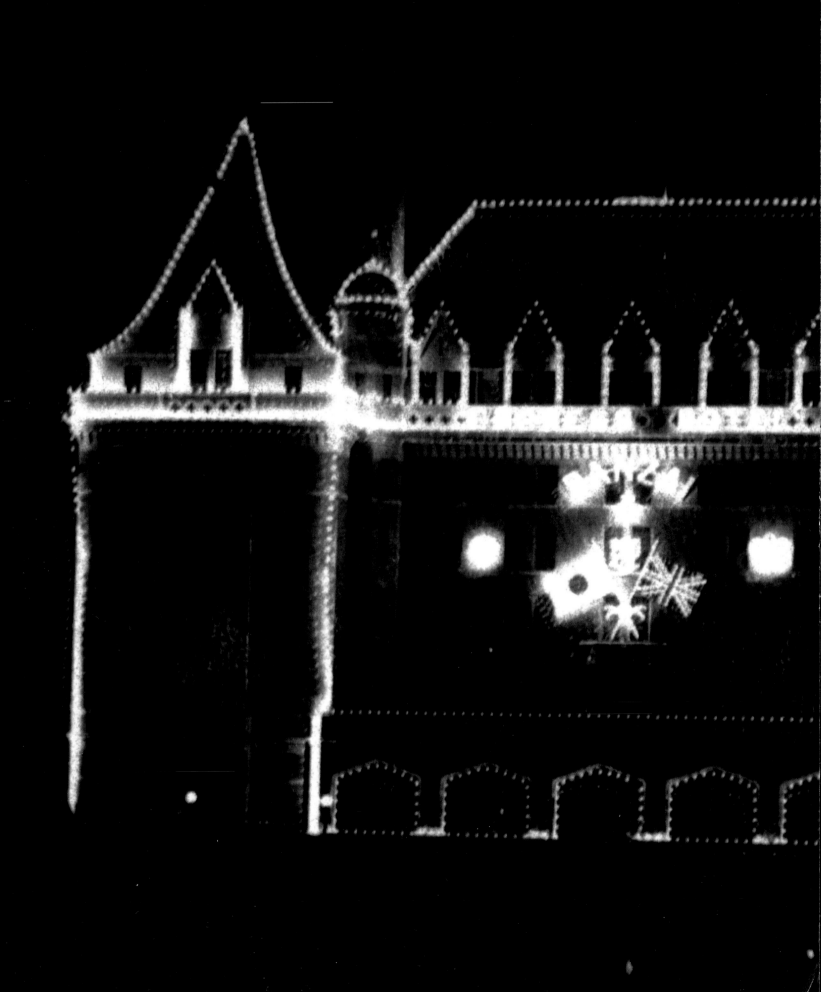

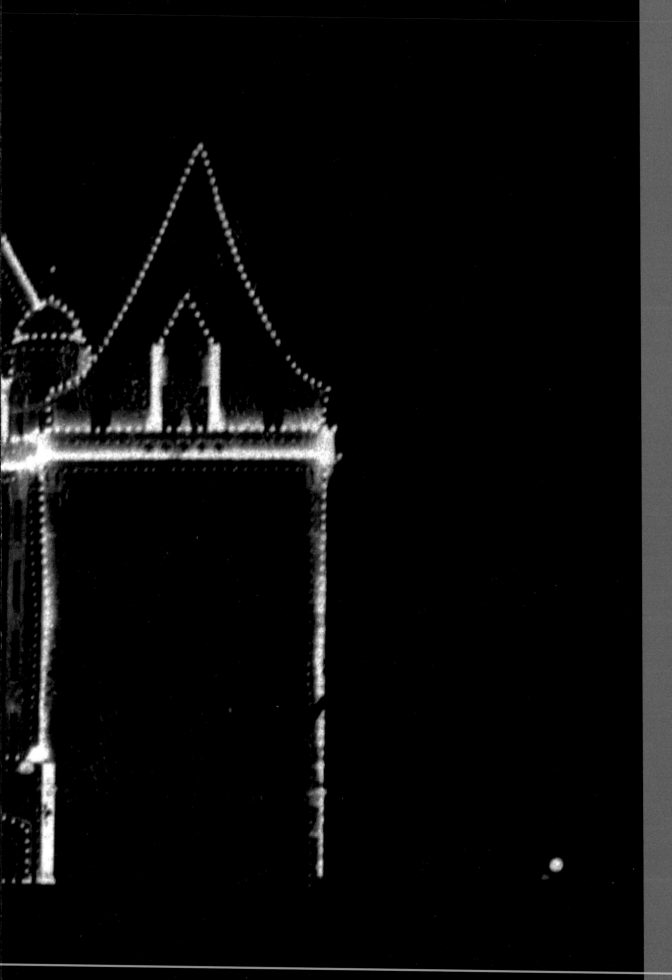

In June 1907, more than six
months before opening day, the
Empress Hotel was outlined
in 2,500 electric lights to mark
the visit to Victoria of Prince
Fushimi of Japan.

B.C. ARCHIVES B-04741

*Chapter One*

# AN OUTPOST OF EMPIRE

ON 20 JANUARY 1908, at the gentlemen's luncheon that marked the official opening of the Empress Hotel, Clive Phillips-Wolley acknowledged his introduction as "the poet laureate of British Columbia" and rose to his feet to proclaim, "This is a wedding feast. Victoria has been waiting long for her Prince Charming. She has been sleeping for half a century. The Canadian Pacific Railway has finally roused her. Victoria waited for the kiss of love and now comes into her own."

It all sounded rather silly, and there were some Victorians who believed that the CPR's "kiss of love" had been delivered by a seducer rather than a suitor. But, even so, there was truth lurking within Phillips-Wolley's overblown metaphor. For while Victoria might not have been "sleeping," it was certainly true that the city was in danger of drifting into a deep economic decline, due in part to its isolated, island location.

By 1908, no one intent on city-building would have considered the southern tip of Vancouver Island an ideal location. But, in the spring of 1842, when James Douglas sailed from Fort Vancouver, the Hudson's Bay Company's trading post on the Columbia River, he had a more modest goal in mind. He was looking only for a suitable site on which the Company could establish a new fur-trade fort, a fort capable of becoming the HBC's western headquarters should the Columbia

River, and Fort Vancouver, fall into American hands.

After exploring several bays and inlets along the island's rocky shore, Douglas decided that a place he called "Camosack" offered advantages he had found nowhere else, including a supply of fresh water and a protected inlet deep enough to accommodate the HBC's supply ships. Construction of Fort Victoria began the following year. Cedar logs were driven into the ground to form a palisade, enclosing warehouses, storerooms and two large residences, one for the Chief Factor, the officer in charge of the fort; the other for the "bachelors," the young men of the officer class who served under the Chief Factor.

In 1846, the Oregon Boundary Treaty fixed the 49th parallel, rather than the Columbia River, as the dividing line between American and British possessions in the west. Now that it was in American territory, Fort Vancouver was gradually abandoned; its role as the HBC's western headquarters was transferred to Fort Victoria; and James Douglas was moved from the Columbia to fill the role as Chief Factor.

Within a few years, the availability of cheap land in Washington and Oregon was encouraging rapid population growth in the American territories. The government in London, aware that it might become increasingly difficult to exercise a paper claim to an almost empty land, developed a plan to encourage British immigration. In 1849, the Colony of Vancouver Island was formed and Fort Victoria became its capital, the home base for colonial governors appointed by the Crown.

But immigration to the colony was slow. Fort Victoria seemed destined to doze on, a quiet backwater, an almost forgotten outpost of Empire. Then, in the spring of 1858, rumours reached California that gold had been found along the Fraser River on the British Columbia mainland, and thousands of "49ers," men who had panned for gold along the banks of the Sacramento River, decided to head north.

Upwards of twenty thousand people streamed into Fort Victoria during the last seven months of 1858. Many gold seekers only paused on their way to the gold fields, but some chose to remain in town to speculate on land or to "mine the miners" by opening businesses. In six short weeks during the summer of 1858, more than two hundred buildings appeared around the fort. "In the morning there will be bonny green grass, at night there be a house on it," an observer noted. The fort's palisade became an impediment to progress, and down it came. "Shops, stores and wooden shanties of every description, and in every direction, were now going up, and nothing was to be heard but the stroke of the hammer and chisel."

In many ways, gold-rush Victoria resembled an American town. "It is the San Francisco of 1849 reproduced," a visiting journalist reported. "The same hurry-scurry, hurly-burly, dirt, dust, inconvenience, bad living, bad housing, cheating and lying."

Each fall, when the mainland gold creeks began to freeze, the town's permanent residents braced for the arrival of overwintering miners. Many of the sojourners were American and, although Victoria was the capital of a British colony, they must have felt quite at home. Businesses like the California Saloon and the Sacramento Restaurant lured them

TOP *Victoria was founded in 1843 as a Hudson's Bay Company fur-trade fort. The fort's southwest bastion stood at the corner of Wharf and Courtney Streets.*
VICTORIA CITY ARCHIVES

BOTTOM *Five months after this sketch appeared in the* Illustrated London News *on 26 August 1848, Fort Victoria became the capital of the Colony of Vancouver Island.*
MCPHERSON LIBRARY, UNIVERSITY OF VICTORIA

TOP *The discovery of gold on the Fraser River in 1858*
*transformed Victoria. In the space of a few short months, the isolated*
*fur-trade fort became a bustling boom town.* PRIVATE COLLECTION

BOTTOM *With its planked sidewalks and false-fronted buildings,*
*gold rush Victoria resembled towns in the American west.*
*The two-storey brick building served as the jail and courthouse.*
*Public hangings took place in the courthouse yard. The area*
*depicted is now known as Bastion Square.* B.C. ARCHIVES A-2640

with familiar names. And the city itself, with its planked sidewalks, its false-fronted buildings and its many saloons was all but indistinguishable from the gold-built towns along California's "Trail of '49."

Victoria escaped the casual lawlessness that typified some boom towns. The rule of British law was firmly in place before the gold rush began and, from the beginning, British rule was supported by the men of the Royal Navy's Pacific Squadron which, since 1854, had been based at Esquimalt, a few miles west of the town. In addition, the town's businessmen and the colonial legislature were both prepared to adopt a pragmatic approach when it came to entertaining overwintering miners.

Knowing that many miners found amusement in the bawdy houses along Kanaka Row, but also aware that not every Victorian would approve of legalizing prostitution, they chose to license them as "dance halls." The euphemism fooled no one. "They are sinks of iniquity and pollution," the *British Colonist* thundered. To which less-fevered minds responded, "Better to have a few sinks of iniquity than have the whole town turn into a cesspool."

Actually, Victoria was already pretty much of a cesspool. There was no sewerage system. Outhouses and privies were sited for their users' convenience, with little thought given to neighbourly aesthetics. Public bathhouses released soapy streams of waste water onto the streets, and cesspools often overflowed into the drainage ditches that lined the roadways. "The gutters in the main streets are at times choked with putrescent filth," the *Colonist* scolded.

The state of the roads was another source of complaint. In the winter, the streets became a quagmire. During dry summer months, the town was choked with clouds of swirling dust. Available water was scarcely enough to quench the thirst of the populace, and, at three dollars a barrel, far too expensive to use to sprinkle the roadways. "Liquor was cheaper than water," a miner recalled. "We remember on a hot day in July seeing a perspiring man enter a saloon to ask for a glass of water. 'Water!' gasped the astonished barkeeper. 'Why, stranger, I'll *give* you a glass of rum, but two bits is the price of water at this yere bar.'"

The lack of water presented a more serious problem than dusty streets. Like any wood-built town, Victoria was vulnerable to fire. The colonial government had taken care to protect its own interests, siting government buildings on the south side of James Bay, a safe remove from any civic conflagration. But with its straw-filled stables and with its hotels, dance halls and saloons lit by candles or oil lamps and heated by woodstoves, the town was in ever-present danger.

Some kind of civic order was long overdue. On 2 August 1862, the colonial legislature passed an Act of Incorporation, and, two weeks later, the first civic election was held. The successful mayoral candidate, Thomas Harris, a 300-pound mountain of a man and the proprietor of the town's first butcher shop, appointed a "Committee of Nuisances" whose job it was to poke about town and be appalled at what they found. Based on the committee's report, the city's first bylaws included such strictures as, "No person shall sink any privy, vault, or cesspool nearer than two feet from his neighbour's premises and not less than twenty feet from the street."

Victoria was in no danger of becoming a health spa, but at least there were *some* regulations governing rapid growth. Two years later, it hardly mattered. By 1864, the best claims had been staked, the readily available gold had been sluiced into pans and poured into bags, and the flood of gold seekers who had worked their way up the Fraser River and into the Cariboo had turned into an ebb tide of discouraged men.

That winter, Victoria experienced "a great falling off of business." Property values plummeted; buildings begun in the spring were left unfinished. The following winter, merchants were forced into bankruptcy as the population, which had once peaked at 8,000, fell to 3,500.

Victoria might be experiencing "general despondency and depression," but on the mainland the situation was even worse. The Colony of British Columbia, with its capital at New Westminster, had been formed in 1858 to ensure British authority over the gold fields. After the collapse of the gold rush, the colonies of Vancouver Island and British Columbia continued to exist as separate entities, each with its own capital, its own governor and its own legislature, and each with its own crippling debt. In order to cut costs, the colonial office in London determined that the two colonies should become one. On 6 August 1866, Queen Victoria put her signature on the Act of Union.

When Victorians read the terms of the act, they were dismayed. Vancouver Island was not being united with British Columbia—it was being annexed. Although Vancouver Island was the senior colony, the governor of the new colony would be Frederick Seymour, the former governor of the mainland colony. The two legislatures would be combined and would meet at New Westminster while the question of a permanent site for the capital was considered. That decision was left to Governor Seymour, who was known to favour New Westminster and whose mind was otherwise clouded by "his constant application all day to spirits." If the governor chose New Westminster, then Victoria might very well become just another gold-rush ghost town. For two years, while Victoria's fate hung in the balance, Seymour dithered. In the end, he ducked the question, leaving the final decision up to the legislature. In 1868, the legislature chose Victoria, and the town's residents sighed with relief and prepared for a future as the capital of the Colony of British Columbia.

A year later, the colonial legislature began negotiating union with the Canadian provinces in the east. In 1871, British Columbia became the fifth province of the Dominion of Canada, and

*By the turn of the century, Victoria was known as a city of beautiful homes and gardens. Grand homes, such as Burleith (this page) and Gisburn (opposite), set in extensive grounds with tennis courts and croquet lawns, lent the city an aura of grace and ease, suggesting to travellers that Victoria would be a pleasant place to visit.*

B.C. ARCHIVES 23592

AND D-3846

Victoria became a provincial capital.

During the 1870s, the town's population levelled off at just over three thousand. The business district, overbuilt during the gold rush, remained confined to a few square blocks, and downtown buildings began to take on a "weather-beaten, antique appearance."

But the cloud of depression that settled over the town was not without a silver lining. As an inducement to enter the Canadian confederation, British Columbia had been promised a railway, a transcontinental rail line to link it to the eastern provinces, and Victorians considered it a foregone conclusion that their town, as the provincial capital, would become the western terminus.

In addition, Victoria was the home of the wealthiest and most powerful men in the province. Poised for the city's railway boom, they consolidated their assets, relished their position as the province's aristocracy and made plans to build suitably imposing homes.

The railway, which had been promised within two years, was a long time coming. It was not until 1880 that the agreement was signed committing the Canadian Pacific Railway to building the transcontinental line. And then, to their horror, Victorians discovered that the dominion government was quite prepared to agree with the CPR's contention that the continent ended on the mainland. By 1882 it was official. The railway would not be extended to Vancouver Island. Victoria would not become its western terminus.

There was some impassioned talk of Vancouver Island separating from British Columbia and seceding from Canada, but in the end cooler heads prevailed. After all, Victoria was an established city,

the largest in the province, and it was the only town that had developed a solid manufacturing base.

While the CPR was laying tracks across the prairies and through the Rockies, Victoria experienced slow but steady growth. The population reached ten thousand and continued to creep upward. Gradually, the tired wooden gold-rush buildings were replaced by stout brick business blocks. Victoria continued to be known as "the largest and wealthiest city in the province," and residents remained complacent even after the CPR's trains began steaming into Vancouver. But the federal census of 1891 brought home an unpleasant truth. When the previous census had been taken ten years earlier, Vancouver had not existed. Now its population had reached almost fourteen thousand, only two thousand fewer than Victoria's. The future had become clear. Nothing could prevent Victoria from sliding into second place.

Vancouver was on the mainland; it had a better harbour, and it was the terminus of a transcontinental rail line. As they watched their industries slipping away to the mainland and as Vancouver's commercial importance continued to grow, residents of Victoria began to think about a future that

Completed in 1898, the new
Parliament Buildings
"anchored" the provincial capital
in Victoria. The architect,
Francis Rattenbury, later
designed the Empress Hotel.

B.C. ARCHIVES D-2772

would minimize their city's geographical disadvantages and maximize its obvious assets.

Victoria was the seat of government, and, as illogical as it might seem to have the capital on an island, there it would remain. The government was housed in the old colonial buildings that had been built during the gold rush on the south side of James Bay. In 1892, the provincial government announced plans to spend $600,000 to construct new legislative buildings on the same site.

Victorians, satisfied that the capital was now "anchored" in their city, made plans to launch themselves into the blossoming new industry of tourism. The goal was simple. Victoria would become "the leading health and pleasure resort of the Pacific Northwest."

Some steps had already been taken to make Victoria more appealing to leisured travellers. In 1889, the city council had voted $25,000 to tame the natural landscape of Beacon Hill Park with the addition of winding pathways and artificial lakes.

Out at Oak Bay, Charles Virtue had opened a seaside hotel, three miles removed from the convenience of the city but providing its guests with beautiful views and healthful breezes. The Dallas Hotel had been built near the outer wharf to accommodate passengers on the *Empresses*, the Canadian Pacific Railway's sleek white-hulled liners that had begun to call at the city in 1891, carrying passengers from Yokohama, Shanghai and Hong Kong. And in the heart of town, the Driard, which had begun its life as a modest gold-rush hotel, had recently undergone a major renovation, including the construction of a new wing that had added two hundred rooms.

On the coast, the Driard had few rivals; in Victoria, it was in a class by itself. According to Emily Carr, who was born in Victoria's James Bay district in 1871 and who later became one of Canada's foremost artists and writers, "Victoria's top grandness was the Driard Hotel; all important visitors stayed at the Driard." Another long-time Victorian guessed that the Driard's renown was due to the excellence of its kitchen. "I have known commercial men to arrange their trips west just that they might stay over in Victoria a day or so to enjoy the meals which were served at the Driard."

But Victorians were hoping to attract a different class of traveller. And, everyone agreed, before the city could seriously promote itself as a health and pleasure resort, something had to be done about the James Bay mudflats, the stinking tidal garbage dump at the city's very doorstep.

In earlier days, the mudflats had offended only when the tide went out and the air became rank with the aroma of rotting seaweed and thick with the heavy smell of drying clam beds. But, by the turn of the century, other elements had been added to the potpourri. The mudflats had become the city dump. "There was no rubbish heap anywhere else. Everything was dumped into the water—old bottles, tins, cans, stoves. Garbage and every mortal thing was dumped there." Adding to the problems were William Pendray's factories, a hodgepodge of buildings strung along Kanaka Row on the north side of the bay, in which he manufactured soap, vinegar and paint. Taking advantage of the water at his back door, Pendray released into James Bay all the noisome waste produced by his various manufacturing processes. "It looked like foam of some kind. He'd just let it run out of the soap-works right into the water, and it'd go backwards and forwards with the tide."

The stench rising from the flats convinced Victorians that some kind of action was desirable; the condition of the James Bay bridge made it imperative. Victorians had good reason to take the safety of their bridges seriously. In 1896 the city's Point Ellice Bridge had collapsed into the waters of the Gorge, carrying with it an overloaded streetcar. The death count had been appalling. Fifty-five men, women and children had been killed, crushed by falling timbers or trapped in the submerged streetcar and drowned.

After the city engineer described the James Bay bridge as a "tottering structure," residents became so concerned that schoolboys being marched across it were warned to break stride "so as not to cause the bridge to fall down."

In July 1900, a group of businessmen gathered at city hall to hear the Tourist Association's Herbert Cuthbert describe a proposal to replace the old bridge with a permanent roadway. The mudflats would be filled to the height of the new road and would become "a pleasure ground and winter garden." Twenty-two shops would line the east side of the road, and the entire roadway would be roofed in glass to form a protected shopping gallery. And all this, Cuthbert explained, could be completed without costing the taxpayers a penny. In fact, an annual profit of at least $25,000 would be produced by the rents paid by the shops and by those who provided "attractions" on the pleasure grounds.

Victoria's mayor, Charles Hayward, studied the proposal with the same methodical sobriety that had made him the town's most successful undertaker. Rather than risk civic dollars on a

*When the new Driard Hotel opened in 1892, it was described as "the most comfortable, and one of the most commodious establishments of the kind in the country." It continued to be Victoria's "top grandness" until the completion of the Empress Hotel.* VICTORIA CITY ARCHIVES 98205-31-4542

speculative enterprise, Hayward decided to put the weight of his office behind a more modest and more cautiously realistic proposal. A permanent roadway would be built and the mud-flats would be filled in, but there would be no glass-roofed shopping gallery, neither would there be a pleasure ground. Instead, the reclaimed land would be subdivided into sixty-one building lots. The sale of those lots would produce revenues of $100,000—precisely the amount the city engineer estimated the work would cost.

In June 1901, when the issue was put to the ratepayers, Dr. Fagan, the city's medical health officer, threatened to "look upon every vote cast against it as a disgrace to the intelligence of the city." Weary after months of discussion and debate, and alarmed by Dr. Fagan's description of the flats as "an absolute menace to health," over one thousand ratepayers voted in favour of the bylaw while only 197 risked the doctor's scorn to register their disapproval.

Within a month, a pile driver was at work pounding 52-foot-long railway ties into the mud in an attempt to find bottom. And the most important civic project in Victoria's history was underway.

The entire project was in the hands of the city engineer, thirty-three-year-old Charles Topp, who had arrived in the city only three years earlier and whose reputation as a "painstaking and capable engineer" was based solely on his design of the civic drains in Chatham, Ontario. Topp would be responsible for every phase of the work, acting as design engineer, super-vising engineer, contractor and clerk-of-the-works.

To hold back the tide, a temporary cofferdam—two rows of piles driven deep into the mud, lined with heavy planks and then filled with mud—was built across the bay below the bridge. The work provided endless hours of entertainment for Victorians who lined the bridge to watch the progress and to comment unfavourably on Topp's expertise. "What are you building a thing like that for?" they demanded. "It'll never hold!" To which Topp responded, "The damn fools! What do they know about it?"

On the evening of 26 November 1901, during an extreme low tide, the last section of the dam was closed, and Topp kept vigil through the night as the tide rose. That morning, residents

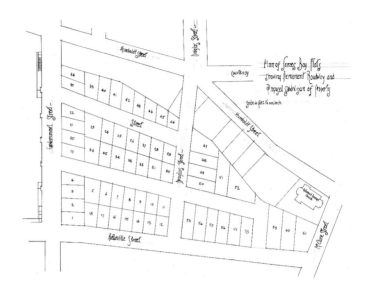

Victoria's mayor suggested that the reclaimed James Bay mudflats could be subdivided into building lots. Kanaka Row (named after the Hawaiian employees of the Hudson's Bay Company) appears under its official designation of Humboldt Street.
DRAWN BY M. J. WYATT, BASED ON A SKETCH IN THE VICTORIA COLONIST, DECEMBER 1900

OPPOSITE TOP The James Bay bridge spanned the mudflats (here the tide is in) to connect the city's legislative precinct with the business district. To the left (under construction) is the post office, completed just before the turn of the century. The tall building in the centre is the Driard Hotel. B.C. ARCHIVES 77954

OPPOSITE BOTTOM The James Bay mudflats were described as "an absolute menace to health." Residents complained that when the tide went out, it left "acres of filthy black slime." John Weiler's furniture factory (centre) later provided the "fancy wood" for the Empress Hotel.
B.C. ARCHIVES 77953

TOP LEFT *By the autumn of 1901, the reclamation of the mudflats was well underway. Below the bridge, a cofferdam held back the sea while 800 wooden pilings were driven to form the foundation for the retaining wall.* B.C. ARCHIVES D-03978

TOP RIGHT *After the cofferdam was closed, the mudflats were drained. The pilings for the retaining wall were sawed off at low water level and covered with a six-foot layer of rock mixed with beach gravel and concrete.*
B.C. ARCHIVES A-04767

OPPOSITE BOTTOM *Another row of pilings, driven parallel to the cofferdam, provided a roadway for the travelling derrick that swung the heavy granite blocks of the retaining wall into place.* B.C. ARCHIVES D-03977

ABOVE *By May 1902, the construction of the retaining wall had reached the halfway point.* B.C. ARCHIVES D-06363

were greeted by a message from the city engineer. Strung across the bridge was a large white linen banner carrying the words: AND THE DAM HELD.

With the dam in place, the condition of the mudflats became even worse. "No tide came in to sweep away Kanaka Row's refuse," Emily Carr remembered. "Smells got frantic and stank to high Heaven."

The city's sanitary engineer did not think that the situation was all that bad. "The dump on the James Bay Flats has been attended to and kept in good condition, the filthiest parts of the rubbish being sent to the bottom and the cleanest parts being spread on top," he cheerily reported.

As the mudflats dried, work began on the causeway retaining wall. By the summer of 1902, the wall was in place, and the work of filling the flats could begin. The level of the mudflats had to be raised almost 20 feet to match the height of the old bridge. It was an immense undertaking, requiring some 210,000 cubic yards of fill, or about 300,000 tons. The only machine capable of that kind of effort was the dominion government's dredge *King Edward*.

One hundred and twenty five feet long and with a crew of seventeen, the *King Edward* could accomplish the filling in about three or four months, but it was busy dredging silt from the lower Fraser River and would not be available until the summer of 1903, a year after the wall had been completed.

"At present the bridge and its surroundings look as though a tidal wave, a mud slide and a cyclone had struck simultaneously," the *Colonist* grumbled. "We should like to know from some reliable authority in what year of the 20th century there is a likelihood of its being completed."

After enduring two years of noise and disruption, Victorians had lost their enthusiasm for the project, and with no end in sight, they evinced little curiosity about the possible use to which the nine acres of reclaimed land could be put. The notion of subdividing the land into building lots had been dropped, and the mayor had taken to describing it simply as "a civic asset." But at least one Victorian recognized that the reclaimed mudflats could become the single most spectacular building site in the city.

Architect Francis Rattenbury had already designed one "ornament" to James Bay, the new Parliament Buildings. Now, he had his sights set on adding another. And he had a particular client in mind—the Canadian Pacific Railway.

*Chapter Two*

# THE TOURIST HOTEL

**E**VER SINCE DECEMBER 1901, when rumours first reached Victoria that the CPR might build a tourist hotel in the city, the Board of Trade's hotel committee had been in hot pursuit of the railway's president, Sir Thomas Shaughnessy.

Dancing before their eyes were visions of Quebec City. In many ways, the two cities were similar. Both were capital cities in somewhat isolated locations. Both were being overshadowed by larger commercial and industrial centres—Quebec by Montreal, Victoria by Vancouver. In 1893, the CPR had built a hotel in Quebec, the Château Frontenac, and after that, the city had gone from strength to strength. As one Victoria alderman put it, "Ten years ago that city was practically dead, but today it is one of the finest and most prosperous cities in the Dominion. The whole character of the city has been changed by the influence of the CPR hotel there."

What the CPR had done for Quebec, it could do for Victoria. With that thought in mind, the hotel committee was happy to note that the CPR had already been taking quite an interest in their city. Since 1891, Victoria had been a port of call for the CPR's *Empress* liners. Then, in January 1901, the company had acquired a controlling interest in the Canadian Pacific Navigation Company with its fourteen coastal steamers and promised to pay particular attention to improving the Victoria-Vancouver run.

*Ships of the CPR's* Empress *line began calling at Victoria in 1891, carrying passengers from Shanghai and Hong Kong and other ports across the Pacific. The* Empress of India *was 455 feet long and carried 120 saloon passengers with 600 in steerage.* B.C. ARCHIVES A-09476

*The fastest and most elegantly appointed coastal steamer in local waters, the* Princess Victoria *was built by the CPR for the Vancouver-Victoria run. Architect Francis Rattenbury designed the interior.*

B.C. ARCHIVES A-00124

In addition, the CPR was, most decidedly, in the hotel business in the west. In February 1901, Victoria's Francis Rattenbury had been selected as architect for the CPR's western division and had revealed the company's decision to spend $400,000 on improvements to the Hotel Vancouver. And he would soon be at work on additions to the company's mountain hotels, including Mount Stephen House, the Chateau Lake Louise and the Banff Springs Hotel. All this activity suggested to the committee that the CPR was finding the hotel business very profitable.

Every time an *Empress* liner docked at the city's outer wharf, a *Colonist* reporter clambered aboard to interview the saloon passengers. And the Board of Trade was reminded once again that the *Empresses* were delivering to their doorstep just the kind of well-heeled traveller they hoped to attract. The problem was, there was very little to encourage them to interrupt their journey at Victoria. The Mount Baker Hotel had burned down in 1902, and its replacement was smaller and more rustic. The Driard Hotel, some ten years after its major renovation, was beginning to look out of date, heavy with the red plush and mahogany of a former era. "To sit in the crimson plush armchairs in enormous front windows and gaze rigid and blank at the dull walls of the opposite side of View Street so close to the Driard Hotel that they squinted the gazer's eyes . . . was surely worth a visit to the capital city," Emily Carr teased.

As they pored over the passenger lists and realized that the likes of Sir Thomas Jackson,

recently retired manager of the Hongkong and Shanghai Bank, and Charles Pulham Clinton, a big-game hunter who had been practising his skills in India, were slipping through their fingers, the Board of Trade's hotel committee made plans for Shaughnessy's arrival in Victoria.

In August 1902, when the CPR president checked into the Driard, they were ready. Accompanied by Mayor Hayward, they "waited on" Sir Thomas and pointed out the advantages Victoria offered as a location for a first-class tourist hotel: mild climate, scenic drives, beautiful homes and gardens, and an aura of ease.

So confident were they that the CPR would see the rightness of their arguments that they had taken the precaution of optioning the best building site in the city, the nine-acre garden attached to James Douglas's former residence on Belleville Street.

The Douglas garden, everyone agreed, was an excellent site, the best the city had to offer. But Francis Rattenbury knew better. The best site the city had to offer was the land behind the newly built causeway. He envisioned a truly monumental Inner Harbour, the Parliament Buildings on the right, the Post Office on the left, and there in the middle, atop the reclaimed mudflats, a magnificent centrepiece—the CPR hotel. He began to prepare sketches of a picturesque waterfront lined with impressive buildings and dominated by a chateau-style hotel rising grandly above the causeway.

After months passed with no further word from Shaughnessy, a more influential hotel committee was formed, composed of members of the Board of Trade, the Tourist Association and city council. Charged with preparing "definite proposals" to put before Sir Thomas on his next visit, the committee came up with three alternative suggestions. If the CPR decided to purchase and build upon the Douglas garden, then the city, with ratepayer approval, would exempt the company from taxation for twenty-five years and would, at its own expense, lay out the reclaimed mudflats as pleasure grounds and gardens. If the company decided, instead, to purchase and enlarge

RIGHT *Francis Rattenbury was British Columbia's most prominent architect. Only twenty-five years old when he won the contract to design the new Parliament Buildings, he secured a series of notable commissions, including Government House, the residence of the province's lieutenant-governor.*
COURTESY OAK BAY ARCHIVES

LEFT *Francis Rattenbury's first sketch of the CPR tourist hotel appeared in the* Victoria Colonist *on 3 May 1903. The site of the Douglas garden (now occupied by the Royal British Columbia Museum) lies between the Parliament Buildings (far right) and the hotel.*

PRIVATE COLLECTION

*CPR President Sir Thomas Shaughnessy was described by his grandson Alfred Shaughnessy (writer of many episodes of the British TV series* Upstairs, Downstairs*) as "a man of tremendous determination, energy and drive. He was also ruthless, and a touch arrogant."* CANADIAN PACIFIC ARCHIVES NS.2523

the Driard Hotel, the same tax exemption would apply. If the company should happen to prefer to build on the reclaimed mudflats, then the city would make the CPR a gift of the land.

When Sir Thomas returned to Victoria in May of the following year, the committee members trooped into the Driard's parlour to press their suit. "Now, I understand you gentlemen want to talk to me about a hotel," Sir Thomas said, getting right to the point. "I want to say that our company is very much adverse to going any further into the hotel business."

"At the same time," Sir Thomas continued, and the committee's spirits began to rise, "provided I was prepared to recommend to our company the erection of such a hotel, what cooperation could we expect on the part of the citizens?"

What the CPR could expect, the committee assured Shaughnessy, was the acceptance of any one of the proposals they had worked out over the last few months, and they carefully explained the advantages of each. After studying the three alternatives, Shaughnessy suggested a fourth.

"If the city will supply the site," he said, "and exempt us from taxation and give us free water for twenty years, we will build a hotel."

Elated, the committee thanked Sir Thomas for making a "distinct offer." The mayor had only one small reservation. If the city made the CPR a gift of the land, it might be difficult to win voter approval for other concessions.

"Well, gentlemen, that is my proposition," Shaughnessy said. "Bear in mind that the company is not anxious to go into the hotel business."

The following evening, armed with Rattenbury's sketches and a plan of the mudflats, the committee called on Shaughnessy to ask if the five acres they proposed to give the company would be "satisfactory" to him.

Indeed, the land did seem to satisfy Sir Thomas. But one thing concerned him. Rattenbury's sketch showed a five-storey hotel of 150 bedrooms. That, said Sir Thomas, was far too small. "We would not think of putting up a building of less than three hundred rooms!"

The committee did not stop to think that this was a rather odd thing for Shaughnessy to say, since, for the last two years, he had consistently maintained that it was not in the company's best interest to build any hotel in the city at all. Sir Thomas, it seems, had been playing his cards close to his chest, feigning disinterest until he was content that he had finessed the best possible concessions out of the city. No matter. Victoria was so desperately eager to be made "a CPR town" that few people stopped to think twice.

On 24 August 1903, the city and the CPR reached an agreement. The city promised to convey to the company 5.1 acres (more than half of the reclaimed mudflats); to fill the said land "to the average levels of surrounding streets"; to maintain, in good condition, the streets and sidewalks adjacent to the hotel property; to prevent the construction of any undesirable buildings on the remainder of the mudflats; to supply the hotel with "good fresh water" free of charge for a period of fifteen years; to grant a tax immunity lasting fifteen years; and, last but not least, to grant a liquor licence as soon as the hotel was ready to open.

In return, the CPR promised to build a "first class modern hotel of stone or brick" costing not less than $300,000; to begin construction within one month of the flats being filled to a satisfactory height; to maintain and keep open the hotel for fifty years; and, during that time, to use none of the land conveyed to them for anything other than hotel purposes.

The agreement was put to the ratepayers on 15 September 1903. That night, the mayor dashed off an excited telegram to Shaughnessy. "Bylaw carried by over twenty to one—only eighty-six against—greatest satisfaction over result." To which Sir Thomas responded, "The good will indicated by the vote is a source of gratification to us all here. We shall commence work on the plans immediately."

Two months earlier, the dredge *King Edward*, finally released from the Fraser River, had arrived in Victoria, and, working from six in the morning till six in the evening, had begun to make progress filling the James Bay flats. By the middle of September, 130,000 cubic yards of mud and silt had been dredged from the harbour bottom and thrown on the flats, and it looked as though the job would be completed by the end of the year. With Rattenbury's hotel plans well advanced, it seemed that nothing would prevent construction beginning early in the new year. Then, in November, disaster struck.

The retaining wall was failing. In fact, it was in danger of giving way. For several weeks, passers-by had noticed that the coping stone at the wall's centre was showing signs of movement. Now, it was a full eight inches off true.

All filling operations were suspended while the city engineer, Charles Topp, scrambled to solve the problem. Several rows of closely packed pilings were hammered into place at the wall's weakest point. Above the pilings, he ordered the construction of a huge concrete buttress, 22 feet thick and over 30 feet high, which was itself buttressed with several thousand cubic yards of rock deposited at its base.

The work took over three months. And because the *King Edward* had returned to the Fraser, operations were delayed even longer while another source of fill was located. Eventually, the city had to spend $2,000 to acquire a sand and gravel pit in the Fernwood area of the city. ("There's a good deal of Fernwood under the Empress hotel," residents would later grumble.) After the city negotiated a contract with the streetcar company to deliver the gravel at a rate of twenty cents per cubic yard, the work of filling the flats began again in March 1904. But despite the company working its men in two shifts, from 6:00 A.M. till midnight, progress was slow.

In a very real way, the failure of the retaining wall was to the CPR's advantage, as it alerted the company to study, more seriously than it otherwise might, the design of the hotel's foundation. Acting on the advice of his chief engineer, Shaughnessy decided to consult an expert, C. S. Bihler of Tacoma, who had served as division engineer on the Northern Pacific Railway and who had extensive experience with foundations of buildings on the shores of Puget Sound.

Bihler's involvement, combined with the delay in filling the flats, proved advantageous in another, unexpected, way. From the beginning, Rattenbury had pictured the hotel sitting squarely in the middle of the causeway, but the city's gift had been limited to five acres, which meant that the hotel would be sited off-centre. Now that he was free of responsibility for the hotel's foundation and with construction delayed by the failure of the retaining wall, he took the opportunity to set matters right.

Rattenbury and his friend Harry Barnard, who had recently been elected mayor, put their heads together and came up with a scheme. William Pendray was still operating his soap and paint factory on Humboldt Street. Approached by Barnard and Rattenbury, he agreed that if the CPR was prepared to pay $76,000, then he would be prepared to sell. As for the reclaimed land between the CPR property and Humboldt Street that was still owned by the city, Barnard would simply convince his council colleagues to give it to the company.

On 27 February 1904, on "Mayor's Office" stationery, Barnard wrote a personal letter to Shaughnessy, suggesting the idea. Sir Thomas responded cautiously. "No doubt there would be some advantage in acquiring the property to which you refer, but at first blush I would be inclined to put the additional money into the Hotel."

Barnard's suggestion received a much warmer reception from CPR Chief Superintendent Richard Marpole. "I was always struck by the desirability of setting the building in the middle of the embankment," he advised.

By 22 April, Sir Thomas had made his decision. He wrote to Marpole, instructing him to go "quietly" about acquiring the Humboldt Street property. Within two weeks, Marpole had secured an option on Pendray's land. "And for $60,000 which is $16,000 less than he first demanded," he noted triumphantly.

Meanwhile, Mayor Barnard had won over his council colleagues to the idea of granting the additional city land to the CPR. That left one remaining property, the lot at the corner of Government and Humboldt occupied by the tumble-down Bay View hotel. When the owner refused to sell, Barnard solved the problem by having the city expropriate it.

Ratepayers would be required to approve the new agreement. With the vote scheduled to take place on 7 June 1904, Barnard had a quiet word with Marpole. Victorians needed some assurance that the hotel would actually be built. It might be a good idea for the company to call for tenders for the foundation before polling day.

But that was something Marpole could not do. The whole business of the foundation was turning into a corporate headache. William Tye, who had recently been appointed CPR chief engineer, had reviewed his predecessor's Victoria file and found himself in a state of near panic.

"I wish to enter a protest against the construction of the new hotel at Victoria on the site as it now stands," he wrote. He was particularly concerned over the safety of the retaining wall.

He recalled another railway company's "disastrous experiences" in nearby Washington state. In order to enlarge their property on Tacoma's harbourfront, the Northern Pacific Railway had built a retaining wall and then filled the tide flats behind it. On the land, they built extensive warehouses. "It was thought that these were safe for all time," Tye said. But one night, just a year after it had been built, the wall failed. "The whole thing went out and the warehouses collapsed like a house of cards. They went down so quickly that the watchmen who were in the buildings were drowned."

The conditions at Victoria were similar. "The Company is taking a tremendous risk in putting

up a hotel in such a place," Tye warned. "The filling may remain in place for many years or it may go out in an instant. If the filling goes out, the hotel must of necessity go too. I need not point out what the result would be."

Tye could think of only one solution. The company should take the $55,000 it was prepared to spend on the foundations, add to that the $60,000 it had agreed to pay for additional property, and then use the money to purchase an entirely different site.

He had a particular site in mind. "It adjoins the present hotel site (which could then be used as grounds); the rock crops out on this site and the foundations would be absolutely safe. The site is almost as good. It overlooks James Bay, and is just across the street from the Parliament Buildings. It would afford almost as good a view of the harbor and the city as the site already chosen."

He was, of course, referring to the Douglas garden. And he was describing exactly the proposal the Board of Trade had put to Shaughnessy a year earlier—the CPR hotel on the Douglas property with the mudflats laid out in gardens—a proposal that might well have won Sir Thomas's approval if Rattenbury had not been so insistent about the advantages of the other.

It was not advice Shaughnessy wanted to hear. By now he

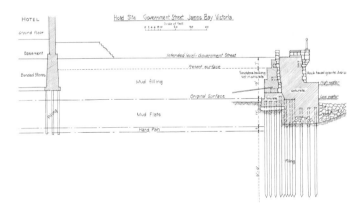

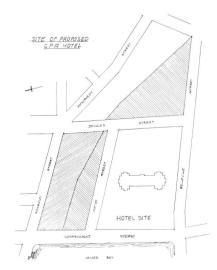

had become quite enamoured of the causeway site. "To my mind the James Bay flats is infinitely the best site for commercial reasons," he said somewhat wistfully. Before deciding to abandon the mudflats, he wanted to consult another expert, E. C. Shankland, a Chicago-based civil engineer.

On 9 July 1904, two days after the ratepayers had trooped to the polls to approve the bylaw granting the CPR the additional land and extending the tax concessions to include all the property from Humboldt to Belleville, Shankland arrived in Victoria and spent several days examining the site. Two weeks later, he submitted a report assuring the company that the city had taken appropriate action regarding the causeway. And as for the hotel, if the changes he recommended were adopted, the foundation would be perfectly safe.

The contract for the foundation was awarded in September to a Seattle Company, Puget Sound Bridge and Dredging, incorporated in British Columbia as the B.C. General Contracting Company. For a price of $80,000, the contractor agreed to an immense undertaking. First, more than 20,000 cubic yards of dirt had to be excavated from the foundation area and deposited behind a temporary cofferdam. Then, almost three thousand 50-foot-long pilings would be driven through the mud, down to the blue clay below. After the caps of the pilings were encased in huge concrete piers, the spaces between the piers and the 25-foot area surrounding the foundation perimeter would be filled with 19 feet of crushed rock, sand and cement.

Laid end to end, the 2,855 foundation pilings would have stretched 27 miles. The concrete for the piers and the foundation floor could have formed a column three feet square and six miles high.

The contractor had no time to lose. Work began on 19 September 1904; completion was required by 1 March 1905. With only five months to go, it was small wonder that he admitted to feeling "up against it." He soon had a hundred men at work, day and night, seven days a week.

Almost immediately, he encountered an unexpected problem. The material that had to be removed from the foundation area appeared to be dry, but when his crew began to excavate, they found that below a thin crust, it was liquid mud. "It is like ladling soup out of a tureen," the contractor muttered.

Still, he managed to complete the work by the middle of March, only two weeks overdue. And now it was the CPR's turn to feel up against it. The design of the building had not been going well.

In November 1903, Rattenbury had travelled to Montreal to meet with Shaughnessy and Hayter Reed, the manager of the Château Frontenac. The plans he set before them were for a seven-storey hotel with 350 bedrooms. "Reminiscent of the Château Frontenac but more symmetrical in appearance," it would be faced with Haddington Island stone, the same stone he had used on the nearby Parliament Buildings. On the building's main floor, overlooking the harbour, he had included a large hall, paneled in oak and warmed by two "old English" fireplaces. Archways opened off the hall into a glass-domed palm garden decorated in the Chinese style in red and gold. Also on the main floor were a dining room, 50 feet wide and 150 feet long, "nobly and richly treated with paneled ceiling, carvings and frescoes"; an oval-shaped ladies' parlour "decorated and arranged in the Marie Antoinette style"; and a library and reading room with an inglenook fireplace. On the lower, or basement, level were a grill room, a billiard room, and a large Turkish bath

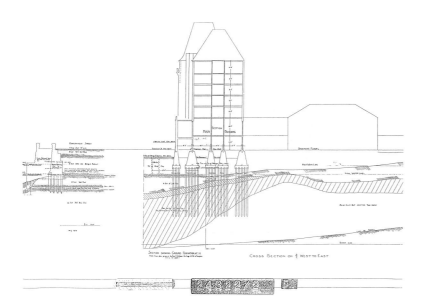

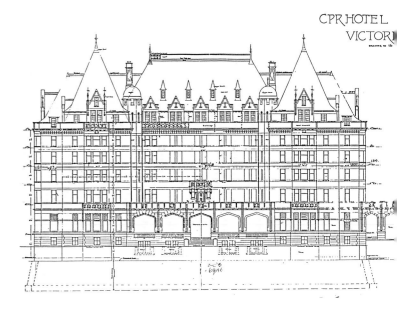

with a lounging room and bar.

The hotel was designed in two sections. A U-shaped centre block, with the palm room in the centre, held all the public rooms, with 175 bedrooms on the floors above; a rectangular wing, running across the top of the "U" and enclosing the palm garden, contained an additional 175 bedrooms.

Rattenbury took careful notes and revised the plans, incorporating all of Reed's suggestions. On 7 May 1904, the new drawings were ready. Following the hotelman's advice, he had included plans only for the centre block. The bedroom wing could be added later, as demand grew.

On 26 May, he received a devastating telegram from Shaughnessy. "Plans very incomplete and proposed arrangement will require good many alterations. Returning them to you with memorandum today."

The memorandum was from Hayter Reed, who had studied the amended plans and sent Sir Thomas eight pages of recommendations and criticisms. Some of Reed's criticisms were minor, but one suggestion Rattenbury found intensely irritating. Reed was proposing a complete rethinking of the ground floor:

> I feel confident that the place would be more attractive if the dining-room were on the floor above that on which it is now placed, with a drawing-room off it, as in the Château. . . . With the drawing-room upstairs overlooking the sea, it would be a great feature. As it is now, ladies coming down in evening dress by staircase or elevator have to go through the long hallway to reach the dining-room. This under many circumstances would be objectionable . . . this Hallway would be used by frequenters from town, which certainly would tend to lack of privacy.

Rattenbury could not have agreed less. The city people would frequent the bar, billiard room

LEFT *In August 1904, CPR engineer George Webster prepared plans for the Empress Hotel's foundation based on the recommendations of E.C. Shankland, an American engineering expert.* COURTESY G. OVSTAAS

RIGHT *Plans for the west—or front—elevation of the Empress (then referred to as "the CPR hotel").* COURTESY G. OVSTAAS

*The specifications for the hotel foundation called for 2,855 50-foot-long wooden pilings. Later, a myth grew that an exotic wood, such as Australian gumwood or eucalyptus, had been used, but tests performed in the 1980s revealed that the pilings are, in fact, Douglas fir.*
VICTORIA CITY ARCHIVES

and grill room on the lower level, he protested. There was nothing to draw them upstairs to the hall.

"I hope Mr. Reed will not press the change, for it means simply throwing all the present working plans aside (now that they are all complete) and beginning again with new sketch plans, just where we were last November."

Being just where he had been in November 1903 was not a place Shaughnessy wanted to be. With the CPR hoping to open the hotel in eighteen months' time, in December 1905, Rattenbury was allowed to win the argument. A few months later, when he provided a detailed description of the interior to a waiting Victoria public, it was essentially the same design. The most important change was the addition of a second grand staircase, closer to the dining room, so that lady guests could descend elegantly to dinner without being observed by the prying eyes of the *hoi polloi* who might have gathered in the hall.

A reporter from the *Victoria Times* to whom Rattenbury confided his plans was quite overcome by the grandeur of it all. "Everything about it will be in keeping with the high class of trade to which the house will cater," he gushed. "When the hotel is completed Victoria will boast a hotel second to none in the Dominion of Canada."

But to build a hotel that would be second to none would cost more, much more, than the CPR had contemplated. The tenders were opened on 16 January 1905. The lowest bid was from A. E. Barrett of Seattle. At $513,433, it was far higher than Rattenbury's earlier estimate of $350,000. Only the architect greeted the figures with equanimity. The price worked out to less than twenty-six cents a cubic foot, he pointed out, and for a fireproof building that was "very low."

With the foundation contractor beavering away to meet his deadline, the CPR scrambled to find ways to reduce Barrett's estimate.

The hotel would be framed in steel, but $20,000 could be saved if the walls were built of wood rather than brick. "A seven storey wood constructed building would burn up in a few minutes, should it catch fire," Rattenbury protested.

Fireproofing could be limited to the first three floors for a saving of $40,000. "It would not be a fire-proof building," he pointed out. "The insurance would be much higher."

The palm garden could be abandoned for a saving of $8,000. "It would be ridiculous to omit this to save $8,000," Rattenbury said. "I don't think it could be put back, as must ultimately be done, for $20,000."

On 2 March 1905, Sir Thomas Shaughnessy brought the debate to an end. "Now that we have undertaken to build a hotel, I do not want to spoil it," he said. If the work could be done for $465,000, then it could go ahead.

Most of the cost reductions came from minor changes—cheaper bathroom fixtures, and the use of wood instead of marble for floors in the public rooms. The largest saving involved the facing of the building. The original tender had called for stone. Now, the building would be faced in brick.

"This change will mean a big difference in the wage bill of the employees on the building," the *Colonist* complained. "Instead of money being paid here for dressing the stone, the money will go abroad to the manufacturers of pressed brick."

One of the arguments used to encourage Victorians to support the hotel bylaws was the amount of local work its construction would provide. Now, it seemed as though the project would not supply as much employment as originally supposed. On 17 March 1905, the contract was let to A. E. Barrett of Seattle. The pressed brick required for the facing was not a commodity that local brickmakers could supply. And there was talk that the contract for the steel had been awarded to "an eastern firm."

The enthusiasm Victorians felt for the CPR's hotel began to wane. But then, in May and June, the news improved. The Seattle contractor had formed a partnership with a local firm, Gribble & Skene, and a Victoria brickmaker, M. Humber & Sons, had won the contract for supplying 2,750,000 building bricks. The CPR's Victoria stock began to rise once again.

By the middle of June, the concrete foundations had set "as hard as any rock." Bricks from the Humber kilns had begun to arrive at the site. Massive steel girders were being hauled into place. Huge blocks of granite, some of them 15 feet long, 8 feet wide, 4 feet thick and weighing as much as 10 tons, had been deposited near the south end of the causeway.

"The renewed activity at the hotel site has greatly pleased the citizens, hundreds of whom go down daily to the flat to watch the workmen piling up the material as it arrives," the *Colonist* noted.

Soon a fence was built from Humboldt to Belleville and "a citizen's eye applied to every knothole."

With local feelings assuaged and with progress on the building now evident, the CPR settled down to the pleasant business of selecting a name for the hotel that had, until then, been known as the Victoria hotel or the CPR tourist hotel. Victorians, asked to contribute their ideas, rose to the challenge.

Rattenbury primed the pump with a few suggestions of his own. The "Douglas Arms" had a certain appeal, he said, but it was "the sort of name usually adopted by places of lesser consequence." The "Royal Oak" was a possibility, but through constant use had lost something of its dignity. The "San Juan de Fuca" had been suggested, Rattenbury continued, but it was "rather too much of a mouthful," and besides, it had other "euphonic objections."

"Something must be settled, and that before long," he warned. The hotel would be finished and open for business by the spring of 1907.

Suggestions flooded in. The "Camosun" to recall the Songhees name for the Gorge. The "Alexandra" in honour of the Queen. The "Van Horne" to commemorate the CPR's first president. The "Lotbinière" after British Columbia's current lieutenant-governor. The "Carnarvon." The "Dufferin." The "Bulwer." The "Lytton." The nominations seemed endless.

On 19 September 1905, Sir Thomas pulled the plug. "The Empress," he decreed. "That will be the name of the hotel."

"An appropriate, majestic title," the *Colonist* agreed. What other name could be more fitting, evoking as it did the great days of the British Raj when Queen Victoria had been named Empress of India and identifying the hotel with the CPR's *Empress* line, sailing between the west coast and the Orient? No one could dispute the choice. Only "The Empress" would do.

By the summer of 1906, the framework for the roof was in place and the roofing slates had been delivered to the site. Plastering of the interior walls was about to begin and the Weiler brothers' factory on Humboldt Street had stockpiles of "fancy wood" waiting for the carpenters. Rattenbury could still feel confident in predicting an opening by May of the following year. But then, in September, Hayter Reed arrived in town and much of the work ground to a halt.

Reed had retired from his position as manager of the Château Frontenac to become the CPR's manager-in-chief of hotels, and he was determined not to miss this last opportunity to put his personal stamp on the new hotel, especially so since his wife, Kate, had been awarded a $10,000 contract to decorate its interior and his brother-in-law, Stewart Gordon, had been selected as its first manager. Accompanying the Reeds and the Gordons on their tour of inspection was Walter Painter, an American who had recently been appointed architect-in-chief of all CPR hotels.

Painter had already studied Rattenbury's plans and suggested changes that Sir Thomas had rejected out of hand. But during his September visit, he managed to come up with some new ideas.

The brick building, which had formed part of Pendray's paint factory and in which Rattenbury intended to place the power plant, should be demolished and replaced by a new building. The refrigeration plant should be moved from the powerhouse to the hotel basement. The addi-

OPPOSITE TOP *Early in 1906, work began on the second floor. This view shows the north side of the building. The arched doorway in the basement level was the entrance that city people were expected to use.* VANCOUVER PUBLIC LIBRARY 469

OPPOSITE BOTTOM *Floors were laid as the building rose. Concrete was poured over a carpet of wire similar to "barbed wire without the barbs."* VANCOUVER PUBLIC LIBRARY 475

tion of an enclosed exterior staircase on the east wall would allow staff to travel from the upper floors to their dining room without having to pass through the kitchen. In addition, Painter felt that the smoking room should be converted into a ladies' parlour and that the manager's office should be moved across the lobby hall and placed on the building's south wall.

When Rattenbury was informed about Painter's recommendations, he could barely contain his rage. A new building for the power plant would cost $40,000 rather than the $15,750 estimated by Painter. The refrigeration plant could not be placed in the basement; the basement provided only nine feet of headroom while the plant required thirteen. The kitchen-staircase addition he found "a Hideous excrescence." And as for the ladies' parlour, Rattenbury's original plans had included just such a space, but Reed had objected to it. "The ladies parlour will not be attractive as the tendency these days is not to be cut off," Reed had advised in May 1904. The plans had been changed accordingly—and now, two years later, Painter wanted it back!

The notion of moving the manager's office, Rattenbury found particularly objectionable. To do so would include "The gutting of a considerable part of the ground floor, removing partitions already built, altering a great number of the Electric light pipes which will necessitate punching many more holes through the concrete floor, the removal of a number of stacks of pipes which will have to be pulled down from the entire height of the building. And all for what? The Manager's office would certainly get an outside view onto the gardens—and that is all."

The company should seek a third opinion, Rattenbury advised. With that suggestion, Richard Marpole was inclined to agree. "Doctors generally disagree among themselves. Our experience proves that Architects have a similar failing."

But the CPR was not required to consult another architect. After mulling the issue over, Rattenbury decided to take drastic action. "I can see no reason, or at the very best a very inadequate reason, for the very sweeping changes that Mr. Painter proposes," he said. "It is my belief that the interior of the building will be much injured, considerable cost entailed, and the completion of the structure delayed without any advantage being gained."

TOP *By June 1906, work was beginning on the sixth floor. The contractor, Gribble and Skene, and E. G. Prior, the local company that supplied the structural steel, were proud of their association with the hotel.*
VANCOUVER PUBLIC LIBRARY 480

BOTTOM *A view of the east elevation in June 1906 suggests how the Empress dominated its surroundings. In Victoria, it was second in size only to the Parliament Buildings. (See page 12, bottom, for an earlier view.)* EMPRESS HOTEL ARCHIVES

On 30 October 1906, he wrote to Marpole. "It is with great regret that I retire from the direction of the completion of the Hotel."

The CPR had no hesitation in accepting his resignation. "If Mr. Rattenbury refuses to supervise the alterations suggested by the Company's architect, at the instance of the Company, then some other architect must, of course, be employed to do it," Sir Thomas decided.

Time was fleeting. Work on those parts of the hotel which involved Painter's suggested changes had already been suspended for more than a month. The planned opening date of 1 May 1907 had already been pushed back to June.

By December 1906, George Dillon Curtis, a Vancouver architect who had done some previous work for the company, had accepted the commission and was in Montreal conferring with Painter. And the CPR was placing responsibility for the delay squarely on Rattenbury's shoulders. "The trouble has arisen over the original plans not being adhered to," the company informed the local press.

With Reed and Painter now firmly in charge and expecting no resistance from Curtis, work should have proceeded apace. But, by the beginning of February 1907, the *Colonist* was still reporting that no work was being done on the ground floor "pending instructions from Montreal."

It was not until 22 March 1907 that the tenders for the new powerhouse were opened. "There is at present a little difficulty," Hayter Reed admitted a few days later. The "little difficulty" was the cost of the powerhouse; the lowest estimate was in excess of $50,000—even more than Rattenbury had predicted. Reed found himself recommending a return to the earlier plan.

On 3 May 1907, a crew set to work to demolish the old chimney of Pendray's building, and Victorians were treated to a most diverting spectacle. Deciding that the best course would be to pull the chimney down, the work crew chipped away bricks at its base, in the direction they wanted it to fall. Next they attached a rope near the top, and an eleven-man tug-of-war team positioned themselves on the high side of Humboldt Street and pulled. The chimney fell just where they had calculated it would, on an open section of the mudflats that had only recently been filled. "The result," an observer reported, "was astounding."

"Tons of mud and ooze were lifted by the impact of the falling bricks. It flew over a hundred yards, splattering the eleven who had tugged so manfully on the rope. The chimney disappeared in the mud. Not a brick of it could be seen."

"The Empress will open on Dominion Day, July 1st," the company announced later that month. To which the *Colonist* was moved to respond, "There will have to be some pretty tall hustling between now and then."

By June, a crew from Otis-Fensom were installing the elevators; plumbers, plasterers and carpenters were crawling over the building; furniture, ordered months earlier, was beginning to arrive; a consignment of rugs was biding its time in storage on the outer wharf. But Dominion Day came and went, and still the hotel did not open.

By the middle of August, most of the rooms on the upper floors were ready to receive furniture and landscapers were at work on the grounds. "Practically everything is complete except the ground floor," Reed admitted.

*By the summer of 1906, the porte-cochère was taking shape and the steelwork for the roof was being put in place.*
VANCOUVER PUBLIC
LIBRARY 486

*Boldly outlined against the sky, the Empress made a great impression on passengers lining the decks of steamers entering the harbour. The hotel became etched on visitors' memories as the one building, above all others, they identified with Victoria.* VANCOUVER PUBLIC LIBRARY 492

In October, the lobby floor was being sanded when Rudyard Kipling arrived in town and was given a tour of the building.

"The hotel was just being finished," Kipling wrote. "The ladies' drawing-room . . . carried an arched and superbly enriched plaster ceiling of knops and arabesques and interlacings, which somehow seemed familiar."

" 'We saw a photo of it in *Country Life*,' the contractor explained. 'It seemed just what the room needed, so one of our plasterers, a Frenchman, took and copied it. It comes in all right, doesn't it?' "

Meanwhile, the *Herald* in Quincy, Illinois, was bursting with local pride. A Quincy carriage-maker had been given the contract for supplying the Empress's hotel coach. "It is all shining in piano finish, with yellow running gear, and solid brass mountings, and the inside upholstered in leather of the most expensive kind," the *Herald* boasted. "It is on ball bearing wheels, with a capacity for 20 persons inside, and five, with the driver, on the fancy cresting-surmounted top. This magnificent coach, as the big gold lettering tells, is for the new Empress Hotel, a $1-million structure at Victoria, B.C., not far from Puget Sound. The new Empress Hotel will attract the world's great, who will ride the new coach to the many natural beauty spots near Victoria."

That was exactly the kind of publicity that Victoria's Tourist Association had been praying for. But the "world's great" would have to cool their heels for a few more months. In mid-October, when Sir Thomas Shaughnessy arrived to inspect the building, it was apparent that the official opening was still several months away.

"It will look very well when finished," Sir Thomas said. "But it will cost too much. That is the only thing."

*Part Two*

# THE EMPRESS OF VICTORIA

*Passengers on the deck of CPR
Princess steamers entering the
harbour were greeted with an
unforgettable view of the
Empress Hotel.* EMPRESS
HOTEL ARCHIVES 16419

*Chapter Three*

# FINISHING TOUCHES

**I**T SHOULD HAVE BEEN A GALA DAY. The twentieth of January 1908. "The opening of the Empress hotel marks a new era in the history of Victoria," the *Colonist* predicted. There should have been fireworks, a parade, a brass band. If the mayor had realized how important a role the hotel would play in the city's future, he would have declared a civic holiday. Instead, the hotel's long-delayed opening was something of an anticlimax.

Hayter Reed had decided that the first official function to be held in the Empress Hotel would be a lunch for fifteen CPR ticket agents and thirty-five newspapermen from Oregon, Washington and British Columbia. It was a jolly, men-only affair, with compliments and congratulations and toasts all round. In a speech punctuated by hearty laughter and rounds of applause, the CPR's irrepressible publicity man, George Ham, set the tone:

The CPR will take you and care for you from the far East to the far West. You can go under the CPR flag from Liverpool to Hongkong, half the circuit of the world—always provided you have a ticket.

Under that great man William Van Horne, and now under Sir Thomas Shaughnessy, the policy has always been to give the public the best of everything; give them everything good and hot—except ice-cream and Scotch.

Later that afternoon, a small ceremony was held when the guest register was opened, with the honour of being the first to sign going to Mrs. Gordon, the manager's wife. And then, at seven in the evening, the dining room doors were thrown open and the public was invited to enter.

At 10:30 that night, Hayter Reed wired Sir Thomas with news of the day's events. "The opening with the press and the CPR agents was a great success and this evening the dining room was crowded to repletion. About one hundred were refused admission. On all sides the greatest praise is being given for not only the building but the dinner and service … The guests demanded to wind up with a dance which is now going on."

It was a magic evening, with an orchestra playing as couples in formal dress floated across the Lounge and drifted into the Palm Court for coffee and conversation. "Can you *believe* we're in Victoria?" they asked one another.

The Empress Hotel was in a class by itself. In Victoria, there was simply nothing to compare to the Lounge, in which Victorian-era fussiness had been banished to create a room that was light and airy and fashionable. Nothing to compare to the Dining Room with its exotic woods and richly decorated ceiling. Nothing to compare to the Palm Court and the quality of the light filtering through the stained glass of its dome. No hotel in the city was set in such extensive grounds and no hotel provided guests with such a view of the harbour.

*The Empress in 1908, with the kitchen wing on the left. The necessity of buttressing the retaining wall resulted in the causeway balcony and boat-landing.* CANADIAN PACIFIC ARCHIVES, COURTESY J. RYAN

The Dining Room was considered the "most gorgeous" of all the hotel's public rooms.
The ornately carved ceiling, which drew so much praise, was actually moulded plaster
painted to look like wood. CANADIAN PACIFIC ARCHIVES 16414

OPPOSITE *Warmed by two large fireplaces and providing a magnificent view of the harbour,
the Lounge was imposing yet still managed to be described as "light and cheery."
Each pillar carried a double band of beaten brass holding four electric light fixtures in the form
of Rocky Mountain sheep heads, designed by Walter Painter.* B.C. ARCHIVES A-02825

The Palm Court, considered by architect Francis Rattenbury to be an
essential ingredient in the Empress's appeal, was dominated by a stained-glass dome.
In this view, the Lounge is to the right. In 1912, the windows on the left were
sacrificed to the construction of the Crystal Ballroom. VICTORIA CITY ARCHIVES

# PORTFOLIO
## *The First Fifty Years*

Panoramic view of Victoria, British Columbia, showing the Provinc[e] Parliament Buildings, the new Canadian Pacific Hotel "The Empres[s] The Dominion Post Office and Custom House, with the C. P. R. "Fly[er]" Princess S. S. Victoria lying at the wharf.

1. TOP *This panoramic post card dates from 1908. The steamer on the right, berthed at the CPR Marine Terminal, is the Princess Victoria. In the foreground is her chief rival, the American boat Indianapolis, owned by the Puget Sound Navigation Company. The large building on the left is the post office.* COURTESY B. SWINDELL

2. BOTTOM *Even before its official opening, the Empress Hotel became one of the most popular post card images of Victoria.* EMPRESS HOTEL ARCHIVES

THE HALL, "THE EMPRESS" VICTORIA, B.C.

3. *The original colour scheme of the Lounge was cream and green with touches of rusty red—a far cry from the dark panelling and heavy red plush with which older hotels were decorated.* COURTESY G. RADFORD

Dining Room, the New C.P. Railway
"Empress" Hotel, Victoria, B.C.

4. *The hotel's green colour scheme was carried through
to the Dining Room.* COURTESY G. RADFORD

# PACIFIC COAST TOURS
## THROUGH THE
# CANADIAN ROCKIES

"THE EMPRESS" VICTORIA

· VANCOUVER · VICTORIA ·
BELLINGHAM · NEW WESTMINSTER
· SEATTLE · TACOMA ·
PORTLAND · LOS ANGELES ·
· SAN FRANCISCO ·
## CANADIAN PACIFIC RY.
1911

# PACIFIC COAST TOURS
## THROUGH THE
# CANADIAN ROCKIES

MT. STEPHEN, CANADIAN ROCKIES

· VANCOUVER · VICTORIA ·
BELLINGHAM · NEW WESTMINSTER
· SEATTLE · TACOMA ·
PORTLAND · LOS ANGELES ·
· SAN FRANCISCO ·
## CANADIAN PACIFIC RY.
1911

npress Hotel and Tally-Ho, Victoria, B. C.

5. OPPOSITE *CPR promotions benefited all of Victoria's hotels and contributed to the boom the city experienced before the First World War.* PRIVATE COLLECTION

6. ABOVE *The Empress shortly after the completion of the south wing. In the foreground is the hotel's six-horse tally-ho, produced by a carriage-maker in Quincy, Illinois, to the CPR's specifications.* COURTESY G. RADFORD

At C.P.R. Docks, Victoria, B.C.

7. *The CPR's first marine terminal was designed by Francis Rattenbury and built in 1904 for $8,900. Most Victoria hotels sent a carriage to meet the steamers. The one pictured here belonged to the King Edward Hotel.* COURTESY G. RADFORD

C.P.R. Landing Place, Victoria, B.C. Canada.

8. ABOVE *The second marine terminal, built in 1924 and designed by Rattenbury with the assistance of Percy James, was a more imposing structure than the first. Rattenbury described it as "a handsome little-building, as good as any I have ever done."* COURTESY G. RADFORD

CRYSTAL GARDEN · VICTORIA B·C

9. OPPOSITE *Inspired by Francis Rattenbury and with working drawings produced by Percy James, the Crystal Garden boasted the largest heated salt-water indoor swimming pool in the British Empire. Victoria's traditional May 24 holiday was postponed to coincide with the Crystal's opening in June 1925.*
PRIVATE COLLECTION

10. TOP *A Conservatory was added adjacent to the hotel's Crystal Ballroom in 1929.* COURTESY G. RADFORD

11. BOTTOM *During the 1930s, CPR promotional material emphasized Victoria's mild climate.* CANADIAN PACIFIC ARCHIVES A-6197

CANADA'S EVERGREEN PLAYGROUND

BALMY INVIGORATING CLIMATE

Enjoy Summer Sports the year round in this land of gardens and flowers

EMPRESS HOTEL

VICTORIA BRITISH COLUMBIA

Social centre of CANADA'S EVERGREEN PLAYGROUND Headquarters for WINTER GOLF TOURNAMENT

# THE *Empress* HOTEL
## VICTORIA, BRITISH COLUMBIA

*Greets You With Charming Gardens*

**One of the many paths winding through the Empress Gardens**

12. TOP *During the 1930s and 1940s, CPR promotional material capitalized on the appeal of the Empress gardens.* CPR 1940 BOOKLET, COURTESY J. CRYSLER

13. BOTTOM *Hand-tinting of black and white photographs could produce garish results, but even so, the beauty and peace of the hotel's gardens are still apparent in this view from the 1930s.* CPR 1940 BOOKLET, COURTESY J. CRYSLER

14. OPPOSITE *The hotel's Conservatory with a selection of head gardener Fred Saunders's prize-winning chrysanthemums. During the 1930s, the Empress was famous for its Chrysanthemum Teas, attracting enthusiasts from far and wide.* CPR 1940 BOOKLET, COURTESY J. CRYSLER

A corner of the
Empress Conservatory

Empress
Hotel...
Victoria,
B.C.

EMPRESS
HOTEL–

VICTORIA
CANADA

15. LEFT *Each Christmas, the Empress produced a special menu,*
*"Ye Fare for Dinner," for its Old English celebrations. This one dates from 1939.*
PRIVATE COLLECTION

16. RIGHT *Every day, the hotel's print shop produced a new menu.*
*On 10 December 1941, the most expensive item was filet mignon at $1.25.*
EMPRESS HOTEL ARCHIVES

Everyone who toured the hotel was impressed, the only criticism coming from those who found its decor a touch "too green." The Ladies' Parlour was decorated in pink and grey, with pink chintz curtains, pink roses on a grey carpet and chubby pink cherubs on the broad frieze running around the room above the paneling. But other than that, the hotel's dominant colour was green, from the furniture in the Lounge to the carpets in the bedrooms.

The hotel's decorator, Kate Reed, liked to work with colour—but only one colour at a time, "in the interests of harmony." In decorating the CPR's Royal Alexandra hotel in Winnipeg in 1906, she had declared, "Oh, everything is blue at present." For the Empress, everything was green, and the effect was somewhat overwhelming.

Kate herself began to wonder if perhaps she had gone too far, particularly in the Palm Court. Within a few weeks, she ordered the columns and ceiling moulding repainted in cream, and she decided that the green-painted panels on some of the walls would be improved by the addition of verses. October would find her ensconced among the palms, a pot of white paint in her hand, lettering in the words to a collection of carefully chosen verses, such as:

Whatever the weather may be, says he,
Whatever the weather may be,
It's the songs we sing and the smiles we wear,
That's a-making the sunshine everywhere.
and
No verses 'neath the bough but let it be,
A pot of black and green—two cups,
And she beside me—eating toast and drinking tea,
Oh! this were Paradise enou' for me.

But the colour scheme was only a minor quibble. On the whole, the Empress's guests were unstinting in their praise. The comments of a guest from Toronto were typical. "The Empress is the best, most homelike and delightfully situated hotel it has been my pleasure to visit."

A visitor from California, whose opinions were thought to matter as he was the proprietor of a hotel in Pasadena, said, "I know of no other hotel which can compare to the Empress. It is well worth a visit to the city to see it."

For the residents of the city, it was simply a case of love at first sight. (It was odd, really. Francis Rattenbury and Hayter Reed, while they had disagreed about almost everything else, were at one in their opinion that guests and city people should be kept separate. Rattenbury thought that Victorians could be confined to the Grill Room and Billiard Room on the lower level; Reed had proposed raising the Dining Room and Lounge to the second floor. And yet, from the beginning, the Empress went out of its way to welcome and encourage Victoria's patronage.) Within four days of opening, the hotel established a businessmen's lunch, a three-course feast at the set price of seventy-five cents. Soon a small orchestra was positioned in the Palm Court to entertain ladies and their guests at afternoon tea. And when the organizers of a fancy-dress charity ball asked if they could use the premises, the management was happy to comply.

*A 1912 CPR brochure included a fulsome description of the Ladies' Parlour: "That woman's taste designed this lovely bower, none need be told. There is no hint of discord in the harmonious picture of a room for woman's delight which meets half-way the unspoken wish of dainty ladyhood."* CANADIAN PACIFIC ARCHIVES A.37074

TOP *The Billiard Room was large enough to accommodate five tables, three English and two American.* CANADIAN PACIFIC ARCHIVES A.37073

BOTTOM *Like the Billiard Room, the Grill Room was located on the lower level. It was equipped with a special oven and grill, ordered from New York, that allowed the chef to work in full view of the diners. The Grill Room and its bar became the favourite haunt of politicians and members of the press gallery.* CANADIAN PACIFIC ARCHIVES A.37075

The ball was held in the Dining Room, where Miss Thain's orchestra, tucked into an alcove, played for seven hundred dancers. The Lounge and the Palm Court, with its "cosy retiring places," served as sitting-out rooms, and the Billiard Room, still empty of its tables, became the supper room. "The society event of the season," the *Colonist* sighed. "A most splendid affair."

Soon, the Empress became the setting for almost every social occasion in the city, from flower shows to St. Andrew's Society dinners to meetings of the Lady Douglas Chapter of the Imperial Order of the Daughters of the Empire. And Victorians were asking themselves, "What did we *do* before the Empress was here?"

To Victoria's Tourist Association, the new hotel was an answer to prayer. It was attracting just the right class of people, the wealthy world travellers who had once passed the city by. Now everyone—from Parisian countesses to retired British Army officers who travelled with their valets—was stopping at the Empress and spending time in the city.

Victoria's merchants, quick to realize that they might profit from their custom, took to placing discreet advertisements in the hotel's literature. Government Street retailers promoted their wares by pointing out that they were "only three minutes' walk from this Hotel." And a local furrier calculated that even well-heeled travellers would be drawn to a bargain. "We wish to mention to the Lady Guests of the Empress that Victoria is the headquarters for sealing schooners. *You can save fully 25% on Seal Garments by buying from us.*"

The worst fears of local hotel owners were not realized. Within two years of the Empress's opening, the Driard would be renovated and freshened from cellar to attic. "At the many other good hotels, the order of the day is the same," an observer noted. "The sentiment is one of keen optimism."

And that optimism did not seem to be misplaced. The CPR had improved steamer service to the city beyond all expectations. Since 1904, the *Princess Beatrice*, an elegant little steamer, fitted out like "a gentlemen's club afloat," had been providing a day service between Victoria and Seattle; the *Princess Victoria*, 300 feet long, capable of 20 knots and fitted out like a small ocean liner, had been making a return trip to Vancouver during the day, and running a service to Seattle and back during the night. American competitors had responded by instituting a rate war during which the fare between Seattle and Victoria fell to fifty cents for a return trip.

As for the Empress Hotel, there was no question that it was a success. If anything, it was proving to be altogether too popular. By July of its first year, it was filling to capacity every night. By August, dozens of prospective guests were being turned away, and the CPR was beginning to think about building an addition.

All the foundation pilings necessary to build the bedroom wing had been driven in 1904, on the advice of the Chicago foundation expert, and the first floor of the north end of the wing had already been built to house the kitchen. Still, the company was cautious. When the books closed on 1908, the hotel had taken in $80,000 but had experienced a net loss of $35,000. The CPR knew better than to expect the Empress to turn a profit in its first few years. However, it seemed only prudent to see what the next year would bring before investing more capital.

By December 1909, when it had become evident that the hotel's annual revenues would exceed $200,000, Hayter Reed made the announcement. A five-storey addition, designed by Walter Painter,

containing 68 bedrooms and 48 bathrooms and costing $125,000, would be built over the kitchen.

J. L. Skene was awarded the contract and agreed to push the work as hard as he could to have the rooms ready for the busy summer season. By July, four floors had been completed and he was about to start on the fifth, which would bring the five-storey addition to the level of the sixth floor of the original hotel.

The new wing was being built across the end of the north side of the centre block. As the work progressed, the contractor removed the fire escape at the end of each corridor, "flight by flight." On 11 July, the last thing he did before quitting work was to remove the fire escape from the sixth floor. That night, fifty-year-old Lizzie McGrath, a chambermaid who lived in one of the small rooms tucked into the sixth floor, decided to follow her usual practice of saying her rosary

*Designed as an outdoor lounging room, the hotel's verandah provided sweeping views of the Inner Harbour and the Parliament Buildings.*

VICTORIA CITY ARCHIVES
98205-32-4549

*An Empress Hotel
advertisement for its
businessmen's lunch in the
Victoria Colonist,
24 January 1908.*

on the fire escape. She opened the door, and stepped out—onto nothing. She fell to the floor below, her death foreshadowing an event that occurred two years later.

The summer of 1911 made it clear that it was all but impossible to overestimate the appeal of the Empress Hotel. By the end of the year, the decision had been made to build a second addition, and once again Walter Painter was given responsibility for its design. It was hoped that the new wing would be ready for occupancy for the summer of 1912, but experienced workmen were in short supply. Victoria was in the throes of a building boom.

All of western Canada was experiencing a period of optimistic expansion, due in no small part to the aggressive promotions of the CPR. Vancouver mushroomed, with its population reaching one hundred thousand and continuing to grow, its identity as the province's leading city attracting new industries and investors. Meanwhile, Victoria too was experiencing growth, even while its industrial base continued to shrink.

"Real estate agents recommend it as a little piece of England," Rudyard Kipling commented, "but no England is set in any such seas. To realise Victoria you must take all that the eye admires most in Bournemouth, Torquay, the Isle of Wight, the Happy Valley of Hong Kong, the Doon, Sorrento, and Camps Bay; add reminiscences of the Thousand Islands, and arrange the whole round the Bay of Naples, with some of the Himalayas for the background."

Given that Kipling had already assured his readers, "On a thousand a year pension a man would be a millionaire in these parts, and for four hundred he could live very well," the wonder is

Empress Hotel, Victoria, B.C.

Completed in 1910, the north wing, designed by Walter Painter, added 68 bedrooms but only 48 bathrooms. The two-storey building on the left housed the hotel's powerhouse and laundry. B.C. ARCHIVES F-2106

OPPOSITE The Empress Hotel became the focus of civic celebrations. Here it forms the background for the parade with which Victorians celebrated the 1911 Coronation of King George V. VICTORIA CITY ARCHIVES

FOLLOWING PAGES The Empress Hotel after completion of the 1910 north wing. Given the height of the creeper working its way up the hotel's facade, this view probably dates from the 1920s. EMPRESS HOTEL ARCHIVES 4533

that he did not start a stampede. Especially so since, as Emily Carr put it, "From London dock to Empress Hotel door was one uninterrupted slither of easy travel."

People flooded into the city—wealthy people who had made their fortunes in Winnipeg or Toronto or Montreal; retirees from colonial outposts in the East who were attracted to the city's English air; young men from England out to make their fortunes in the west.

Between 1910 and 1913, five hundred new members joined the Union Club, and the gentlemen members voted to spend $400,000 to build a new headquarters on Humboldt Street. At the corner of Humboldt and Government, a group of local investors began construction of the Belmont Hotel. Plans were being prepared for two new theatres, and the Hudson's Bay Company began building a grand new department store.

Throughout the city, residential construction was proceeding apace. Open land disappeared as cow-yards, orchards and market gardens were swept away to be replaced by brown-shingled houses squeezed onto small lots.

And so, in the spring of 1912, the Empress's contractor J. L. Skene was happy to hire any men he could get. That was good news for twenty-three-year-old Harry Rhyl. He arrived in the city in February and within days was signed on as a builder's helper. At ten o'clock on the morning of 30 March 1912, Harry delivered a load of mortar to a bricklayer working on the sixth floor. Making his way back along the cornice, he slipped, crashed through the wire screen strung around the building to catch falling tools, and plunged down 70 feet to the ground below. Fellow workers who rushed to his aid found "a crushed heap." He died on the way to the hospital.

VISITORS
FREE
INFORMATION
BUREAU

As the second addition was reaching its full height, the contractor made an ominous discovery. The south side of the hotel was sinking. The differential between the extreme northeast and southwest corners was a full 18 inches. That was so alarming a development that the CPR president immediately called in a team of experts from New York.

Westinghouse, Church, Kerr and Company concluded that the problem had arisen when the weight of the new wing, and the weight of the extra fill that had been used to bring the porte-cochère driveway to the required level, had combined to compact the layer of blue clay into which the pilings had been driven. As the clay compressed, it had carried the pilings down with it.

The solution lay in decreasing the load. Four and a half feet of fill was removed from the sub-basement under the southern half of the building. Twelve and a half feet was removed around the perimeter of the new south wing, and the

space created was covered by a concrete deck. The grounds leading to the porte-cochère were excavated a full 20 feet, and again the space was covered with a concrete deck, creating a "relieving chamber," a huge room of air, above which the grounds were cautiously relandscaped. Altogether, the weight of the load was decreased by some 11,000 tons, resulting in a "striking reduction" in the rate of settlement.

By the summer of 1914, the Empress had been completed in a fashion that exceeded architect Francis Rattenbury's vision. Between the two bedroom wings, the hotel now boasted a ballroom, the Crystal Ballroom, a dreamily romantic space with a greenhouse roof that allowed daytime sunlight to sparkle on the crystal chandeliers and nighttime dancers to waltz under the moon and stars.

Already the Empress had lost its raw new look. Along the west side of the building, the vines planted in 1908 had reached the first floor, and dozens of roses had begun to soften the lines of trellises, arbours and pergolas.

And the hotel had begun to show a profit. In 1911, the Empress had taken in $399,000 for a profit of $53,000. The following year, revenues rose to $505,000 for a profit of $106,000. The year 1913 was even better, with revenues rising to $594,000 and profits to $135,000.

For the CPR steamships, business was booming. By 1911, two new *Princess*es, the *Adelaide* and the *Alice*, had been added to the night service between Vancouver and Victoria, and orders had been placed for two new ships, both destined for the Seattle run. In addition, two new *Empress*es, the *Russia* and the *Asia*, had been ordered for the trans-Pacific service.

With the steamship service and liners gearing up to carry ever more visitors to the city, it appeared that the Empress could look forward to years of prosperity. But then everything changed.

The news that Britain was at war with Germany reached Victoria on the afternoon of 4 August 1914. The expectant crowd that had gathered outside newspaper offices, eager for the latest news from Europe, burst into cheers, followed by heartfelt singing of "God Save the King" and "Rule Britannia."

*The Empress's south wing in 1925. The porte-cochère was the hotel's main entrance until 1989.* EMPRESS HOTEL ARCHIVES 16387

OPPOSITE TOP *The second addition to the Empress, the south wing, was completed in 1912. Several rooms wider than the north wing, it marked the first major departure from Rattenbury's design.* CANADIAN PACIFIC ARCHIVES NS.16385

OPPOSITE BOTTOM *The difference between the hotel's north and south wings was more evident on the east elevation. The structure between the two wings is the Crystal Ballroom.* VICTORIA CITY ARCHIVES 98010-03-4743

TOP *The Reading and Writing Room occupied the first floor of the hotel's 1912 addition. During the 1930s, it was presided over by a severe looking white-haired lady who not only chose the books she thought guests should read but also distributed them each morning at ten o'clock from locked-up glass-fronted bookcases.*
VICTORIA CITY ARCHIVES 98302-02-1855

BOTTOM *Added to the Empress in 1912, the Crystal Ballroom featured a daylight ceiling and ten chandeliers, each composed of 8,000 individual crystal beads.* B.C. ARCHIVES F-02126

Throughout the city, men made plans to enlist. Soon, uniforms were everywhere. On the corner of Fort and Government Streets, the 103rd Battalion recruited volunteers from a temporary fortlike structure carrying a banner: "Come and See Sunny Belgium and France with Us." Out at Oak Bay, the Willows Fairground was converted into a military camp where men, recruited from throughout the province, were trained, and then marched through town to the CPR docks to board a *Princess* steamer for the voyage to Vancouver and the beginning of their journey to the Front.

The real estate boom, already faltering, staggered to a halt. Savings and fortunes were swept away as many speculative houses remained unsold. The Hudson's Bay Company halted construction of its new department store, and plans for the Belmont Hotel were abandoned.

Like the city, the CPR felt the impact of the war immediately. The Empress remained the centre of social life in the city, but now charity balls gave way to patriotic fundraising events, and annual banquets to regimental dinners. The *Princess Irene* and the *Princess Margaret*, both nearing completion in Scotland, were requisitioned by the Royal Navy. The *Empress of India* was converted into a hospital ship. The *Empress of Asia*, at Hong Kong when the war began, was requisitioned for use as an armed merchant carrier, and a similar fate befell the *Empress of Japan* and the *Empress of Russia*.

The CPR now had only one ship on the trans-Pacific route, and the effect on the Empress Hotel was devastating. During 1915, the first full year of war, the hotel experienced a loss of $33,000. And the situation would have been even worse if it had not been for the patronage of Americans, still at peace and able to travel but denied the pleasures of Europe. Victoria, "a little bit of olde England," was the next best thing. But soon, America too would be at war, and by then the hotel was already struggling with a strange new phenomenon. The Empress could no longer provide wine and spirits to its guests.

The ability to sell liquor had been recognized as being so important to the hotel's appeal and profits that the CPR's 1903 agreement with the city had included a clause guaranteeing the Empress a liquor licence. In June 1906, with pending legislation threatening to limit the number of licences a city could grant,

Victoria had made good on its promise and issued the hotel a permit, even though the building was eighteen months away from completion.

But now, no special provisions could be made for the CPR. British Columbians had become caught up in a moral and patriotic crusade against "Demon Rum." Succumbing to the blandishments of church and temperance groups with their cries of "Prohibition Means Purity" and "Save the Girls," they voted the province dry.

On 1 October 1917, it became illegal to sell or manufacture any beverage containing more than 1.5 per cent alcohol, the only exceptions being sacramental wine and medicinal whiskey. Breweries and a few saloons survived by selling near-beer, a weak brew known affectionately as "ferret's piss." Distilleries and distributors limped along after doctors suddenly found whiskey to be a magnificent cure for a variety of ailments. But the Empress bar, which had become a favourite haunt of the members of the legislature and the gentlemen of the press, was forced to close, and wine could no longer be served in the Empress's Dining Room.

Eventually, the war ended, and the CPR's *Princess*es and *Empress*es sailed into the harbour, bringing the men home. But nothing was quite the same. Decades would pass before the city experienced the prosperity of the prewar years. Twenty-five years would slip away before the Empress generated profits equal to those produced in 1913. And two generations would come of age before a bottle of wine could be uncorked in the hotel's Dining Room.

From June 1920 to June 1921, the *Empress* liners carried almost ten thousand first-class passengers across the Pacific, an increase of almost 400 per cent over 1914. That increase was reflected in the Empress Hotel's balance sheet, producing an average annual profit of $45,000 for 1920, 1921 and 1923. But there was a financial cloud on the horizon. The concessions granted by the city in 1908 were reaching the end of their fifteen-year term.

CPR officials arrived in the city to argue in favour of extending the hotel's special status. But it was the worst possible time to be seeking civic favours. The city's ratepayers were

TOP *In February 1916, Victoria experienced a snowstorm such as the city had seldom seen. Roads were blocked by six-foot drifts, and stranded residents were forced to tear down fences for firewood to keep warm. The Empress generated its own power, and when the city's supply failed, the hotel became a haven.* PRIVATE COLLECTION

BOTTOM *On 2 April 1919, the Empress was draped with flags to welcome the men of the Canadian Mounted Regiment on their return from the Great War.* VICTORIA CITY ARCHIVES 9903-05-3201

*In this 1920s view, the number of cars and taxis lined up along Belleville Street suggests that a* Princess *steamer has just entered the harbour.* CANADIAN PACIFIC ARCHIVES 10723

staggering under an almost intolerable tax burden. During the prewar boom years, roads had been built, and sewer and water lines laid. Now, with the speculators either bankrupt or long gone, property owners were being forced to pay for a variety of improvements from which they received no benefit. By 1921, properties representing 10 per cent of the assessment roll had reverted to the city for unpaid taxes. By 1922, the city was so short of money that plans were afoot to cease maintaining parks and boulevards and to cut the wages of the men who swept the streets from $4.00 to $3.75 a day.

Beginning in 1923, the Empress would become liable for $22,000 a year in taxes and $9,000 annually for water. When Basil Gardom, the CPR's superintendent of hotels, suggested that the company pay $12,000 a year for both, he was informed by one alderman that there was not "a ghost of a chance" of the city's agreeing to a subsidy of $19,000. There was, however, some room for negotiating.

Victoria had been exploring the feasibility of building a recreation centre, the idea being not only to provide for the amusement of Victorians but also to furnish a lure for winter tourists. A Chamber of Commerce committee, which included architect Francis Rattenbury, had come up with a grandiose scheme. In one glass-roofed building, the "Amusement Centre" would include a heated salt-water swimming pool surrounded by "a huge conservatory featuring palms, exotic plants, ferns, hanging creepers, bright flowers and singing birds." In addition, space would be provided for a dance floor, an art gallery and for "indoor tennis, badminton, bowls, shooting galleries, archery and other wholesome sports."

It sounded quite wonderful. The problem was that the city could not even begin to finance such a structure. But now, in return for concessions, perhaps the CPR could be coaxed into building it.

By January 1923, a deal had been hammered out. The city would set the annual bill for tax and water at $15,000 for 1923 and 1924, during which time the CPR would explore the feasibility of building the amusement centre. The agreement between the city and the CPR required ratepayer approval. At first it seemed as if the bylaw would have little chance of passing. It did not enjoy the unanimous support of council, one alderman describing it as "one of the most monstrous bylaws in the history of the city" to roars of approval from another.

"Some taxpayers are going without the necessaries of life in order to make ends meet," a beleaguered ratepayer complained. "If they cannot afford to pay their water bill it is turned off." How could one justify charging the Empress only $5,000 for water when the hotel consumed more water than the entire municipality of Oak Bay?

To forestall the bylaw's defeat, Victoria's businessmen and the editors of both newspapers launched a publicity campaign such as the city had never seen. Day after day, the editors argued in its favour, and day after day both the *Times* and the *Colonist* ran lengthy interviews with businessmen, who argued that the CPR deserved the city's support and suggested that defeat of the bylaw would result in economic disaster.

Victoria, they pointed out, benefited from the CPR's worldwide advertising campaigns and from the company's "excellent" passenger service to Seattle and Vancouver. The hotel was the city's social heart and its gardens functioned as a public park. The Empress employed about two hundred city residents. And the CPR had made Victoria the headquarters of its coastal steamship service when it could just as well have chosen Vancouver. According to one prominent businessman, the CPR was supporting, directly and indirectly, 25 per cent of Victoria's population.

On 5 February 1923, property owners went to the polls to support, overwhelmingly, the new agreement. Less than a year later, they were back in the voting booths. The CPR had discovered that building an amusement centre was, indeed, feasible.

*Like the Empress Hotel, the Crystal Garden was built on reclaimed land. The building "floats" on a concrete "mattress" 30 inches thick.* CANADIAN PACIFIC ARCHIVES 14761

RIGHT *Crystal Garden brochure.* B.C. ARCHIVES NWP387 C212SP

CRYSTAL GARDEN
VICTORIA, B.C.
REAR *of* EMPRESS HOTEL

FINEST PLACE OF AMUSEMENT ON THE PACIFIC COAST

*Have a Swim, Tea or Dance Between Boats*

The CPR promised that the Crystal Garden would boast the
"most beautiful indoor gardens imaginable" and the "finest salt-water
swimming pool in Canada." B.C. ARCHIVES 63465

TOP *In 1928, the Billiard Room became the Georgian Lounge. Furniture that had been in the main Lounge since 1908 was refurbished and reupholstered and moved downstairs. The Georgian Lounge could be rented for private parties, one way to circumvent British Columbia's strict liquor laws.* COURTESY E. PENTY

BOTTOM *The new-look Dining Room was redecorated in blue and featured a portrait collection of the wives of Canada's Governors General, moved to the hotel from the Royal Alexandra in Winnipeg.* COURTESY E. PENTY

CANADA'S FIRST LADIES

Portrait Collection
IN
THE EMPRESS HOTEL
VICTORIA, BRITISH COLUMBIA, CANADA

LOUISE ELIZABETH, COUNTESS OF DURHAM, 1838

*The portraits of the wives of Canada's Governors General prompted so many inquiries that the Empress produced a booklet providing biographies of each subject.* PRIVATE COLLECTION

OPPOSITE *Designed by CPR architect J. W. Orrocks and built at a cost of $2,500,000, the 250-room Humboldt wing was completed in December 1929. The Government Street elevation contained six luxurious suites, one on each floor. Number 130, the vice-regal suite, can be identified by the height of the ceiling.* B.C. ARCHIVES A-08800

The company would construct a glass-roofed entertainment palace costing not less than $200,000 provided that: the city lease them the land (a two-and-a-half acre parcel across Douglas Street from the hotel) for one dollar a year; exempt the leased land from taxation; supply free water to the amusement centre for twenty years; and, perhaps most important of all, agree to continue the current rates on the Empress Hotel ($10,000 in tax, $5,000 for water) for twenty years.

Enthusiasm for the proposal was high. On 23 December 1923, ratepayers—for the fourth time in twenty years—voted in favour of granting concessions to the CPR. "A great step toward lasting prosperity," the Chamber of Commerce rejoiced.

Victorians would discover that their support had not been misplaced. By the time the Crystal Garden, designed by Francis Rattenbury and refined by Percy James, was ready to open in June 1925, the CPR had spent $308,000 on its construction and decoration. And the city could boast of having the largest heated indoor salt-water swimming pool in the British Empire.

Confident that the Crystal Garden would capture the interest of winter travellers, the CPR embarked on a two-year $150,000 plan to renovate and redecorate the Empress. In 1927 work began on replumbing and rewiring rooms in the north wing, and a new revolving door was ordered for the entrance on Government Street. The following year, the Billiard Room was converted into the Georgian Lounge; the Grill Room was redecorated and renamed the Tudor Grill; the Palm Court became the Tea Room; "new period furniture" appeared in the Lounge; and the stiff, high-backed dining-room chairs were replaced with smaller, daintier models. And the whole colour scheme had been rethought. Now the Empress was predominately blue.

But the changes planned by the CPR went much further. On 26 November 1928, the *Victoria Times* went to press with stunning news. The city's skyline would be "radically changed." The company would build a massive new wing on Humboldt Street, a huge addition to the Empress which would increase the number of bedrooms from 300 to 550. On 21 January 1929, when the contract was awarded to Carter-Halls-Aldinger Co. Limited of Winnipeg, the scope of the project became clear. The new wing would cost $2,500,000. And because it would cover the site of the existing powerhouse and laundry, a new facility would be built, adding $500,000 to the cost.

In a city with fewer than 40,000 inhabitants, an investment of over three million dollars to provide a hotel of 550 bedrooms (580 if the rooms in the suites were counted individually) was nothing short of awe-inspiring.

The official opening—an afternoon tea hosted by the ladies of the IODE—took place on 21 December 1929. When the premier, Simon Fraser Tolmie, threw open the new wing to public inspection, the seven hundred invited guests were nothing if not impressed. Each floor contained a multiroomed suite, and each suite was decorated in a different style, from the light airy look of the Spanish and Italian suites on the fifth and sixth floors, to the heavy oak of the Tudor vice-regal suite on the first.

"The new wing establishes the Empress as one of the world's finest inns," a well-travelled Victorian proclaimed.

TOP *The construction of the Humboldt wing marked the last major change to the exterior until 1989. For sixty years, this was the image of the Empress with which people were familiar.* EMPRESS HOTEL ARCHIVES 10469

BOTTOM *The siting of the Humboldt wing played havoc with the hotel's internal traffic patterns. As the floor plan shows, the Humboldt wing was not built up against the centre block. Instead, the two were connected by a hallway-wide bridge.* CANADIAN PACIFIC ARCHIVES

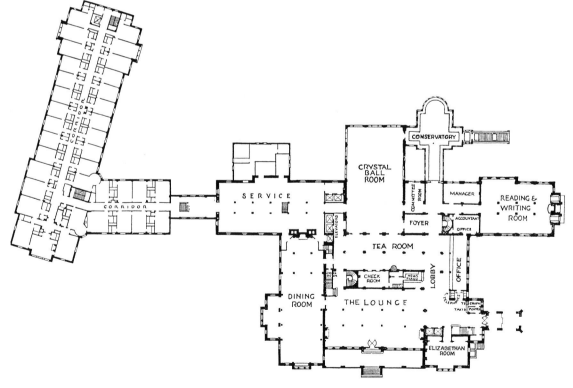

*After the construction of the Conservatory, the Palm Court became the Tea Room. But once the sound-muffling palms were removed, a quiet conversation on one side of the room could be heard clearly on the other, and guests found themselves conversing in whispers.* CANADIAN PACIFIC ARCHIVES 16407

## Chapter Four

# GRACIOUS LIVING

ETWEEN 1930 AND 1935, THE EMPRESS HOTEL built up a net loss of almost $100,000, and for the rest of the decade it managed to produce only a modest profit. And yet, it was during the thirties that the Empress entered its heyday, a time during which innovations became "time-honoured traditions" and the image of the Empress Hotel as the "grand old lady of Government Street"—quaint, rather eccentric and very English—became set, seemingly forever, in the public imagination.

During the 1930s, the Empress gardens came into their own. Head gardener Fred Saunders knew the grounds from bottom to top, having signed on as an assistant gardener in 1908. Except for the three years he spent overseas with the 88th Battalion during the Great War, he devoted his working life to the garden's perfection.

Born in England in 1890, Saunders had apprenticed in the gardens of Gatton Park, the Surrey estate owned by Jeremiah Colman, the "mustard millionaire." In many ways, the gardens he developed for the Empress resembled the grounds of an English country estate, with wide herbaceous borders, wisteria climbing over warm brick walls and arbours and pergolas entwined with perfumed roses. And like an English estate-gardener, Saunders aimed to make the hotel self-sufficient, if not with fruit and vegetables, at least with flowers and decorative plants of amazing variety.

*The gardens played an important role in the Empress's appeal. In 1908, the south driveway
had not been completed, but already the framework for the pergola was in place, and a
start had been made on the rock garden at the corner of Government and Humboldt Streets.
To the rear of the hotel is the powerhouse with its tall smokestack.* PRIVATE COLLECTION

RIGHT *Curving pathways and graceful arches invited visitors to explore the Empress Hotel's extensive gardens.* B.C. ARCHIVES F-02123

LEFT *The Empress Hotel's head gardener, Fred Saunders.* EMPRESS HOTEL ARCHIVES

He developed a nursery garden and a cutting garden, in which he grew delphiniums, evening primroses, sweet peas, lobelias, Michaelmas daisies and dahlias "with blooms as large as soup plates." Under 20,000 square feet of greenhouse glass, he raised everything from seed or cuttings, providing all the bedding plants for the gardens around the hotel and the Crystal Garden. He estab-lished two specialty greenhouses. One was a shaded "fern house," in which he grew amaryllis and poinsettias for the hotel's Christmas celebrations. The other was a "stove house," in which he grew tropical plants, including orchids and "other things of delicate character," all of which would find their way into the hotel's Conservatory or the Crystal Garden.

Part of the grounds were devoted to recreation, with clay tennis courts at the southeast cor-ner and a perennial-bordered putting green on the east lawn behind the hotel. But most of the gar-den was designed for relaxation, with deck chairs spotted here and there among the flowers and with curving pathways inviting afternoon strolls.

The north lawn and the rock garden had been sacrificed to the construction of the new wing, but the lily pond at the northwest corner survived as a cool oasis on hot summer days. "The lake contains water lilies and bulrushes, and is altogether a little gem of landscape gardening," a visi-tor enthused. "And here it is within a few yards of one of the busiest streets of a city."

Compared to later years, the streets surrounding the hotel were blissfully quiet. It required very little imagination for guests to believe that they were wandering through the gardens of an old

*Located near the corner of Government and Humboldt Streets, the rock garden and lily pond offered a cool oasis on hot summer days.* B.C. ARCHIVES H-03460

OPPOSITE *In keeping with the Empress's summer role as a resort hotel, the corner of the garden at Douglas and Belleville Streets was devoted to clay tennis courts.* EMPRESS HOTEL ARCHIVES M3894

English estate. Summer visitors spent more time in the gardens than they did in the Lounge or Tea Room—reading, chatting, taking tea and, on more than a few occasions, holding press conferences.

The Empress's manager, Kirk Hodges, recognized the garden's ability to attract guests. In 1933, he established a Chrysanthemum Tea held during October, at which Fred Saunders and other enthusiasts displayed their prize specimens. The popularity of the Chrysanthemum Teas, attracting over six hundred guests every year, prompted a more ambitious programme. In 1936, the Empress began to sponsor a Spring Garden Festival. Organized by Fred Saunders and Herb Warren, the head gardener in the city parks department, and enthusiastically supported by Victoria's gardeners, the four-day event was held during the first week in May. Drawing guests from as far away as Dallas and Atlanta, the festival included lectures from experts, a flower-arranging competition and a tour of as many as forty local gardens.

Small wonder that the CPR began to describe the Empress as located "amid this garden glory" and, in the 1940s, published "a book of gardens" as a hotel souvenir:

The ivy-clad Empress, set in 10 acres of garden, is the keynote of the garden city and focal point of its garden and social activity.

Its gardens—famous for roses from April to January, chrysanthemums, wall-flowers, tulips, dogwood, alpine rock plants and a myriad other colourful flowers and shrubs—greet you when your fast Princess line from Vancouver or Seattle ties up a short walk from the hotel.

Gardening and social life go together in Victoria. The pleasant city, its atmosphere that of an English country town, entertains in its gardens.

Your own Victoria garden—The Empress Hotel grounds—attracts every kind of

Filled with a fairy fragrance.. the Empress Hotel rose gardens!

*The rose garden, with its "fairy fragrance," was featured in a 1940 booklet. The company's promotional literature described the Empress as being located "amid this garden glory."*
COURTESY J. CRYSLER

floriculturist. Here working gardeners who grow their own flowers can revel in potting sheds, forcing beds, cutting beds—can discuss seeds and bulbs, slips and cuttings—can watch experiments in breeding and the development of new varieties for which The Empress Hotel gardens are noted.

It happened that the inspiration behind one of the Empress's most enduring traditions came from the hotel's gardens.

One of the eight gardeners who worked under Fred Saunders was Major Llewelyn Bullock-Webster. Born in Wales in 1878, "the Major" had been intended for the army but, after failing to pass for Sandhurst, he had thrown himself into the theatre, training as a Shakespearean actor but making his mark in Music Hall with an "equestrian turn" in which he played a character known as "Bronco Bill." By 1928, he was decidedly down on his luck and was making his way by teaching elocution and drama during the winter, and working in the Empress gardens during the spring and summer.

When the Empress's manager began to muse about ways to improve the hotel's winter appeal, Bullock-Webster assured him that something more could be made of Christmas.

The Empress's first Christmas in 1908 had been celebrated in the grand style with a Christmas Eve ball for the staff. The carpets in the Lounge were rolled back; ropes of evergreens, entwined with hundreds of small incandescent lights, were strung between the pillars; and dozens of lighted red Chinese lanterns were hung from the ceiling. In the centre of the room stood a Christmas tree, "the largest ever seen in Victoria," glittering with three hundred electric lights. For the staff members and their guests, who waltzed into the early hours of the morning, there had never been a Christmas to compare.

But since then, the hotel had done nothing out of the ordinary to mark the season. Why not, Bullock-Webster suggested, stage an Elizabethan Christmas celebration, an "olde English" bacchanalia complete with boar's head, Yule log, carols and carousing?

The first "Old English" Christmas was a tentative, toe in the water affair, intended for Victorians rather than visitors. Ten days before Christmas 1928, the event was advertised in local newspapers. For $2.50 per person, guests could expect dinner and dancing and "Full Mediaeval Pomp."

Major Bullock-Webster, a man to whom the grand theatrical gesture was second nature, was given responsibility for organizing the event and delivered rather more than the advertisement promised. As he later reported:

> Those who were at the Empress last Christmas are still talking of the thrill that swept through the great hall when the boar's head was brought in, borne aloft on a platter by a chef in Elizabethan costume, preceded by a jester prancing in cap and bells and followed with pomp by steward and minstrels. They will remember the dragging in of the Yule Log, the wassailers, the exquisite old Nativity Play, the scenes from Dickens, the singing of carols outside the Parliament Buildings, led by Lieutenant-Governor Bruce himself.

Bullock-Webster, who continued to direct and perform in the ceremonies until he was in his seventies, had hit upon a magnificent idea. In 1929, the hotel produced a promotional brochure, and soon guests were arriving from across the continent. By 1939, twelve hundred guests, half of whom were American, were in attendance, and there would have been more if the hotel had not been forced to close off reservations in November.

Many people returned year after year. For them, the Empress's mediaeval celebration became a personal Christmas tradition. Almost sixty years after the Empress's first Old English Christmas, Mabel Wood would be able to count on its ability to draw people back, year after year, to find the love of her life.

Mabel was a spinster, an independent woman who supported herself as an insurance broker in northern California. "I used to go away at Christmas," she recalled. "I just didn't want to get involved in all the family stuff."

One year she decided to spend the holiday in Victoria. After Christmas dinner at the Empress, Mabel listened to the carol singing in the Lounge and then went for a walk. A few steps along the path from the porte-cochère, she heard someone calling her. She stopped and turned to see a tall, square-shouldered, silver-haired man coming toward her. "I saw you in the lounge," he said. "I thought you were waiting for someone, and then I saw you leave alone."

A seasoned solo traveller, well aware of the dangers of chance encounters, Mabel was never able to explain what she did next. Instead of rebuffing him, she let him fall in step beside her. They walked through the deserted Christmas night streets of Victoria. "We talked and talked. It was like we'd known each other forever." The following day, Mabel went home to California.

**EMPRESS HOTEL**
# Christmas Dinner

Served in Main Dining-room, also New Grill at 7:15 p.m.
Concert Orchestra, Main Dining-room
Crystal Garden Orchestra, Grill Room

During Dinner the Old Ceremony of
**Bringing In the Boar's Head**
Will Be Carried Out With Full Mediaeval Pomp With
the Singing of
**The Boar's Head Carol**
And Other Christmas Carols

After-dinner Dancing in the Ballroom for Dinner Guests
(Non-dinner Guests for Dance, $1.00)

**$2.50 Per Person**
Reservations, Head Waiter, Telephone 1680

*Advertisement in the* Victoria
Times, *15 December 1928.*
PRIVATE COLLECTION

"I found I just could not forget this man," she admitted. "There wasn't a day went by that I didn't think about him." By September, she decided to go back and find him.

When she arrived in Victoria on Christmas Eve, she asked if Oscar had checked in. He hadn't. She spent the evening watching television in her room. Christmas Day was bleak and gloomy. She wandered around the Empress, poked about the shops that were open, and then went for a walk. "I didn't want to go back to my room and sit all afternoon," she said. But finally, she returned to the hotel, and as she stepped into the elevator she heard a voice saying, "I know you." She spun around. It was Oscar.

"I'm so glad I found you," he exclaimed. "I thought you might be here." Oscar was in the room next to hers. They had each spent Christmas Eve alone, only a wall apart.

They booked the same two rooms for Easter, and again for the following Christmas. By then, Mabel had decided to retire to Victoria. She moved into a little apartment, and Oscar came over every other weekend. Finally, Mabel said to him, "You know, I don't want to marry you, but I sure would like to live with you."

"It was just perfection from the moment he moved in," Mabel recalled. "We were so hopelessly in love, we were just pathetic."

They had been together for six years, and Oscar was eighty years old, when he was diagnosed with inoperable cancer and given two months to live. He asked Mabel to marry him. He was too ill to get to the church, so they were married at home. "You'll notice I'm not wearing white," Mabel quipped to the clergyman who performed the ceremony.

That night, she told Oscar she had a confession to make. "Honey, I've lied to you. I'm older than you are."

"Yes," Oscar said, "I know that. You're eighty-one, aren't you?"

"Well, no," Mabel said. "Actually, I'm ninety-one."

Oscar died three months later. "You know," Mabel mused, "the funny thing is we never went back there. I guess we just weren't Empress kind of people."

Definitely "Empress kind of people" were the hotel's permanent residents. By the 1930s, they had become recognized as an essential ingredient in the hotel's quirky charm. The first permanent resident was Harry Helmcken, a grandson of James Douglas. Harry and his wife, Hannah, had attended the opening banquet in 1908 and had been so impressed by the new hotel that they had decided, then and there, to quit their rooms in the Driard and move to the Empress.

In those early days, when help was cheap and easy to come by, hotel-living in Victoria was somewhat unusual. But by 1920, the situation had become very different. "After the war, help was impossible to get," an elderly resident mourned. And, as it happened, the city was filling with people who were competing for the services of maids, cooks and gardeners. Working people were deserting the city, but they were being replaced by a "better class" of person—older and richer. By 1931, almost 10 per cent of Victoria's residents were over sixty-five, the highest proportion of any city in Canada.

For the well-heeled retiree who was accustomed to gracious living, making one's home at the Empress made a great deal of sense—maid service, meals on demand, gardens to enjoy, huge public rooms for relaxing or entertaining, an excellent location and a respectable, not to say distinguished, address.

All of those features appealed to Dr. Cecil ffrench and his wife, Florence, when they moved to Victoria in 1920. Born in England, Cecil ffrench had studied veterinary medicine in Montreal and later in Munich, and then moved to Washington, D.C., where, he liked to boast, he had treated Teddy Roosevelt's dogs.

Dr. ffrench had patented an ingenious invention—worm pills for dogs. The idea of enclosing medicines in a gelatin capsule, avoiding the problems of trying to feed liquids or powders to unco-operative animals, proved so popular that he decided to devote his retirement to its manufacture. A short block away from the Empress, he opened a small manufacturing plant, the ffrench Remedy Company. There, he produced his worm pills and a variety of other products, including his own special flea powder, which came with an official-looking document, suitable for framing, certifying that one's pet had become a member of "Dr. ffrench's Flea Free Fraternity."

Meanwhile, his wife, Florence, took pleasure in gliding silently around town and along the scenic drives in her electric car, a tall narrow black brougham, equipped with a bud vase on its dashboard and capable of a maximum speed of six miles an hour.

The ffrenches and the other permanent residents were valued by the management because their presence helped to alleviate the problems created by the hotel's dual role. The Empress was a resort hotel, catering to the summer tourist trade, but unlike the Banff Springs Hotel and the Chateau Lake Louise which shut up tight during the winter, it also functioned as a city hotel. In fact, the CPR's agreement with the city required that it remain open year-round.

During the winter months, it was not uncommon for staff to outnumber guests. And so year-round residents were important to the Empress, as were the increasing number of visitors who escaped from more rigorous climes to overwinter at the hotel. One elderly lady, who made it her habit to move in every autumn and remain until spring, endeared herself to the staff. "She was sweet. A dear old thing. Very gracious, and very, very refined." Always, night after night, she dined alone, always at a table for two just inside the dining room door. And night after night, she repeated the same postprandial ritual. Her meal complete, she delicately patted her mouth with a linen napkin. Next she dipped her fingertips in the finger bowl and patted them dry. Then, she daintily removed her dentures and swished them carefully in the finger bowl before replacing them. That done, she made her way, sedately, to the Lounge for the evening concert.

Almost all of the permanent guests were well off. They had to be. The hotel offered special off-season rates for long-stay tenants, but those rates were far from cheap. From 15 October 1929 to 30 April 1930, a double room with bath and meals cost $375 a month; a similar room without meals was $210—but that was still a small fortune at a time when the monthly wage for a labourer was $80. However, the hotel did issue a tantalizing promise to guests who counted their tenancy in years rather than months: "Special Rates for extended visits upon application."

During the 1930s, with the Great Depression wiping out the investments on which some of the residents lived, rates dropped to as low as a dollar a day for those "Empress dowagers" who were content to live in one of the sixth-floor rooms formerly occupied by staff.

The ladies of the sixth floor, some of whom were not nearly as poor as they thought they were, did their best to economize. One elderly lady became famous for her habit of coming down every day for afternoon tea, ordering a pot of hot water and then producing a tea bag from her purse. Some of the dowagers were said to have smuggled hot plates into their rooms so that they could avoid the expense of eating in the Dining Room. The story goes that one lady made strawberry jam on her hot plate and that another filled the air of the sixth floor with the unmistakable odour of liver and onions.

Publicly, they did their best to keep up appearances. After spending their afternoons playing bridge at the tables set up for them in the Tea Room or the Reading Room, they swept down to dinner in outmoded Edwardian gowns, laden down with their best jewelry.

Accustomed to having the Empress more or less to themselves for much of the winter, they did not suffer tourists gladly, especially tourists who had the temerity to lower themselves into one of the chairs in the Lounge that everyone *knew* was *theirs*.

They became part of the ambience, part of the character of the Empress. Guests, particularly American guests, delighted in their eccentricities and looked for them on their return. One of their most endearing charms was their complete obliviousness to modern taste and contemporary celebrity.

During the late thirties and early forties, the actor Spencer Tracy was a frequent guest, stopping off at the Empress on his way to and from salmon-fishing excursions at Campbell River. On one occasion, he found himself sitting in the Lounge beside an Empress dowager listening to an evening concert by Billy Tickle and his trio. Noticing that heads were turning in their direction, she bent toward him and asked, "Why is everyone looking this way?"

"Don't know," he whispered.

Later that evening, she was approached by a woman who gushed, "I see that you know Mr. Tracy."

"Mr. Tracy? Which Mr. Tracy? I don't know *any* Mr. Tracy."

"Why, Spencer Tracy, of course."

She looked at her sternly. "My dear, I can't think who you are talking about!"

For those permanent residents who believed that gracious living included an occasional sherry or the pleasures of savouring a smoky Scotch, British Columbia's bizarre liquor laws continued to be an obstacle.

In 1919, returning servicemen, many of whom were "notoriously wet," had been quick to point out that a dry province was not on the list of the things for which they had been fighting. In October 1920, voters approved the repeal of total prohibition. Public drinking would continue to be banned. However, wine, whiskey and beer could be purchased from government liquor stores for consumption in private.

Also in 1920, by happy coincidence, the United States embarked on its own noble experiment with the passage of the Volstead Act, which prohibited the sale or manufacture of intoxicating liquors. The following year, when the B.C. government opened one of its first liquor stores on Humboldt Street, a stone's throw from the hotel, thirsty Americans added scotch, rye, rum and gin to their check lists of the Empress's appeal.

But while it was now legal to purchase liquor in British Columbia, it certainly was not easy. Liquor stores kept regular office hours, and to buy even a bottle of beer required a personal liquor-purchase permit. The whole process was so tortuous that tourist-information brochures found it necessary to offer detailed instructions:

> First, obtain permit at any liquor store. Second, look over stock, present your permit to clerk and place your order. Third, present your order to cashier and pay cash. Fourth, present your order to clerk in stock department and have your order filled. Fifth, do not open or remove contents until you have reached your destination.

It was enough to drive a man to drink. Far simpler for a visitor to have a quiet word with one of the taxi drivers waiting for custom outside the Empress. The price would be high, at least double that charged by the government purveyor on Humboldt Street. But for good reason. Supplying liquor to guests was a risky business. The government was employing the services of private investigators whose chief *modus operandi* was entrapment.

Kenneth LaChance and Carl Ledoux were two of the most devoted "liquor spies" in the government's employ. On the night of 7 July 1922, they checked into the Empress Hotel, approached a young taxi driver, John Kershaw, and asked him to get them some whiskey. Within half an hour, Kershaw was knocking at their door with a bottle in his hand. He charged them three dollars. "Well, a dollar of that is for taxi fare," he explained, when they complained about the price. They invited him to have a drink, and before Kershaw's glass was dry he found himself charged with having violated the Liquor Act.

Bellboys and room-waiters ran the same risk of falling foul of government spies, but for them the potential for profit was even higher, making the risk all the more worth taking. They stuffed their lockers with bottles of liquor. Approached by a guest, they would frown thoughtfully, and then admit that while it might be possible, it would certainly be expensive. After all, they were on duty and could not go and get it themselves. A taxi driver, and perhaps a bootlegger, would have to be involved. It would take some time. "So we'd check our watches," one bellboy recalled. "We'd

*Jack Ellett (left) and Jack MacDonald photographed in 1933 wearing the Empress's traditional page-boy uniforms: red jackets with brass buttons, and royal blue pants with a gold stripe down the sides.*
COURTESY J. ELLETT

let about a half-hour pass. And then we'd go to our locker, collect a $1.50 bottle of booze and deliver it to the room for five dollars, saying, 'The bootlegger, the driver—that's why it costs so much.' They'd grumble. But they always paid. And we'd get a good tip for our trouble!"

In 1924, a majority of the province's voters approved the sale of beer, by the glass, in licensed hotel beer parlours. Regulations required that these beer parlours be relentlessly grim. There could be no entertainment, no singing, no card playing. It was simply a case of "sit down, shut up and drink your beer." Even so, the Empress Hotel might have been tempted. But, in Victoria, even beer parlours were outside the realm of the possible. The law was applied constituency by constituency, depending on the outcome of the vote in each individual riding. Victoria's voters had opposed hotel beer parlours, and so, in the city, public drinking of any kind remained strictly banned.

There were ways around the law. Private parties were beyond the regulations. That was the notion behind the decision to convert the Billiard Room into the Georgian Lounge, and other rooms on the lower level into private dining rooms, all of which could be rented for private parties.

The Spring Garden Festival opened with a cocktail party, but the guest list was limited to registrants and the affair was arranged as a private party hosted by the manager. Christmas presented a different problem. By limiting the celebration to registered guests, it could be considered a private party. In that case, liquor could be served, but it could not be sold. Guests had to bring their own. "By Christmas Eve, the maître d'hôtel had taken delivery of the queerest sorts of parcels: old-fashioned pigskin Gladstones, suitcases, boxes, even—once—a string bag, all of which he stowed in his 'speak,'" an employee remembered.

Day in, day out, the Empress's permanent residents had to come up with different solutions. They could, of course, drink in their rooms, and more than a few dowagers were known to keep a secret bottle of sherry hidden in their toilet tanks. Those who enjoyed a drink with their dinner poured whiskey into a flask which they positioned behind the tall, upright menus. "We knew what was going on," a waiter said. "We just looked the other way." (On at least one occasion, they went further than that. In 1929, when Winston Churchill dined at the hotel, he was served his favourite tipple in a china teapot.)

Turning a blind eye was the technique adopted by management to accommodate the drinking preferences of the crowds who came for the Saturday night dances in the Tudor Grill or the special dances in the Crystal Ballroom. Tablecloths, reaching almost to the floor, concealed the shelves that had been so helpfully provided a foot off the ground.

"There was no vulgar flouting of the antidrinking ordinances," Peter Stursberg, a young reporter with the *Victoria Times*, recalled. "While the waiters provided ice and mixes as a matter of course, they insisted that the bottles when not in use should be stowed under the tables."

For big annual dances, like the Policemen's Ball or Firemen's Ball, when the Ballroom was so packed with people that the tables had to be removed, the usual custom was for a group of friends to rent a bedroom to drink in. So well established was the practice that the hotel detective had been known to peer through an open bedroom door, shake his head at the array of whiskey bottles lined up on the bureau and then go silently on his way.

The problem was that many dancers spent more time in the bedroom bars than in the Ball-

room. Peter Stursberg remembered a 1936 debauch that was typical rather than extraordinary:

> It was two o'clock in the morning when Billy Tickle struck up "God Save the King," but the party was beginning to reach a crescendo in the bedroom bars. Our room was full and as frantic as a beehive; a fellow I didn't know was stretched out cold in the bathtub; a couple of babes were doing a soft shoe on one of the beds; a small group was standing with their arms around each other, singing ... The smashing of the glass top of the bureau was innocent enough; one of the self-appointed bartenders just banged a bottle down too hard ... Some of the more inebriated took it as a signal to "break up the lousy joint," but they were restrained. An argument developed as to whether the broken glass top should be left on the bureau, or removed and the shards stacked in the cupboard, or thrown out the window. The moderates, or the moderately drunk, prevailed, although in the heat of the moment, one fellow did toss a pillow from the window.

According to Stursberg, his group had been quite civilly restrained. Other revellers had broken into a fire-fighting station on the second floor and used the axe to break down doors and smash furniture. And several chairs and at least one bed had been thrown from the windows onto the flower beds below.

"The Firemen's Ball and the Policemen's Ball; they were always the worst," page-boy Jack Ellett grinned. "Fire hoses pushed through the windows and turned on. Sheets tied together and people shimmying down from the third or fourth floor."

Provincial politicians, the men who made the laws with which the hotel's guests grappled,

*Gathered on the lawn (c. 1931), the waitresses are wearing the dinner uniforms prescribed by the CPR's Manual of Service Rules: "white dresses; white stockings and shoes, rubber heels at all times; small white tea aprons; soft white collars and cuffs; white caps."* COURTESY S. BELL

*The Crystal Ballroom was the scene of annual galas staged by many clubs and organizations. The 1937 Firemen's Ball was typical—very crowded and very formal. The bedroom barrooms, necessary because of the prevailing liquor laws, were equally crowded but rather less well behaved.* COURTESY D. HART

apparently availed themselves of every dodge the Empress offered. Bruce Hutchison, who covered the legislature for the *Victoria Times* and who liked to claim "more politics are made in the bedrooms of the Empress than in the cabinet chamber," remembered an occasion when "a Speaker of the Legislature, having drunk deep, awakened with a shriek on the slab of an undertaker's parlour where his friends had whimsically dispatched him." And another time, "a politician of note was playfully chucked out an upper-storey window but fortunately landed on a handy roof and rested there comfortably until morning."

Hutchison was not about to name names—a wise move given the Press Club's devotion to rowdy Empress parties. At one annual ball, the club hired an actor to make a communist speech to provide "a mild diversion" for the invited guests. The results were spectacular. "The ballroom witnessed its first riot," Hutchison recalled. "Gentlemen broke one another's noses and women's gowns were torn off."

With the prevailing liquor laws tending to produce roaring drunks rather than moderate drinkers, the Empress walked the tightrope of potential scandal. The hotel detective might look the other way when it came to bedroom bars, but he had no tolerance whatever for any sexual shenanigans. Barney Lane, a seventeen-year-old elevator operator in the late 1930s, had the opportunity to watch him in action. "He used to creep along the halls, pressing his ear against every door. He was determined that no room booked as a single was being used as a double."

That was how the detective caught Gordon Gibson. Gibson later became a self-made millionaire and a member of the British Columbia legislature, but in March 1936 he was thirty-one years old, a tough, hard-driving, hard-drinking young man in need of a holiday. He had spent the last few days battling the weather down from Clayoquot aboard the schooner *Malahat*, a 245-foot-long log carrier. Arriving in Victoria, he booked a room at the Empress and then called a girl friend. After dinner, he suggested that she come up to his room.

Half an hour later, there was a knock at his door. "No overnight guests allowed," the detective sang out.

"We're going out again," Gibson growled.

Another half-hour passed. Another knock. Gibson scrambled into his clothes and went out into the hall. "You leave me alone! This is none of your goddamned business," he yelled.

"Get that woman out of your room," the detective shouted.

Gibson decided "to scare the jesus out of him." He grabbed him, marched him down the hall, threw open the exit door and bent him over the fifth-floor fire escape. "I didn't actually hang him by his feet; I just picked him up and said, 'You son of a bitch, you mind your own business and leave us alone or you're liable to bounce on that pavement down below there.'"

But the detective's determination knew no bounds. Gibson had just crawled into bed with his girl when he returned—with the police—and threw them both out of the hotel.

Keeping scandal at bay, or at least out of the newspapers, was part of the reason behind manager Kirk Hodges's decision to hire the hotel's first press agent. When Gwen Cash took on the job in

January 1935, Hodges made it clear that an important part of her responsibility was "keeping the bad news under cover." The manager was particularly leery about suicides. Not that the hotel was a magnet for suicides, just that they tended to make for the most unpleasant kind of front-page coverage. That had certainly been the case when William Rouch of New York decided to end it all.

He had attracted no attention when he checked into the Empress on 12 May 1923, and over the next few days nothing about him elicited comment. At 5:30 on the evening of 17 May, the housekeeper informed the front desk that she had been unable to get into his room all day. Using a master key, the assistant manager opened the door and found Rouch lying on the floor in a pool of blood. There was a gun, a 45-calibre U.S. army pistol, on the edge of the bed, its handle stained with blood. On the dresser was a letter to his mother, and in the bathroom was a bottle of rye whiskey, three-quarters full. The coroner's inquest deemed his death "suicide while in a state of temporary mental derangement," and there was no suggestion that the Empress had been in any way at fault. Still, the front-page headline, SUICIDE IS VERDICT IN EMPRESS HOTEL DEATH, was enough to make a manager cringe.

Gwen Cash had been on the job for only a few months when her talents at "cooling it" were put to the test. Ernest May, seventy-six years old and a retired banker from California, was not a permanent guest, but he came so often and stayed so long that everyone on the staff knew him. "He was very genteel, very well dressed, a charming old man." He arrived at the Empress in April 1935, intending to stay through the summer. On the evening of 21 June, he plunged from his third-floor window and landed in a heap beside the porte-cochère entrance. He was clad in pajamas. It was possible that he had opened the window and then lost his balance. Kirk Hodges thought otherwise. "Why couldn't he have done it somewhere else?" he groaned. "The old boy always said he loved the Empress."

The location of May's death was described in the press only as "a downtown hotel." Five years later, Cash did even better when faced with a particularly grisly double suicide. A prominent physician from Saskatoon was spending Christmas at the Empress with his wife. On 28 December 1940, they attended the hotel's Saturday night dance. Later that night, after they had retired to their fourth-floor room, his wife "went through the window."

"It was awful," the assistant manager, Bill Reynolds, shuddered. "She had hit a balcony on the way down. There was blood everywhere."

The following day, her husband locked the door to his room, climbed into the bathtub and, with professional precision, used his razor to sever the artery in his groin.

"I didn't drink much," Reynolds remembered. "But I'll tell you, I had a drink that night."

On 30 December, local newspapers described the event as having occurred "in a downtown building."

It happened that the most scandalous affair relating to the Empress Hotel took place a world away. More than any other individual, architect Francis Rattenbury was responsible for the public face of the CPR in Victoria, having designed the original hotel, the Crystal Garden and the company's marine terminal. But by the late 1920s, he had become anathema to the CPR and to the citizens of Victoria, as the result of his extramarital romance with Alma Pakenham—beautiful, giddy and thirty years his junior. He divorced his wife and married Alma, but Victorian society continued to shun them. In 1930, they travelled to England and settled in Bournemouth. Rattenbury began to drink heavily, and Alma found diversion with their eighteen-year-old chauffeur, George Stoner. On 25 March 1935, Stoner, suspecting that Rattenbury had discovered he and Alma were lovers, bludgeoned the Empress's architect to death. Alma and Stoner were charged with murder and stood trial in London's Old Bailey. Acquitted and released, Alma committed suicide. George was convicted and sentenced to hang. Fifty-five years after Rattenbury's murder, Stoner, who had been reprieved and eventually released, was in court once again, convicted of sexually assaulting a twelve-year-old boy.

Equally important in Gwen Cash's role as press officer was getting favourable publicity for the hotel. She began to send photographs taken by the hotel's photographer, accompanied by chatty press releases that included detailed guest lists, to newspapers in visitors' home towns. Some editors were inclined to be cautious, writing to inquire, "Are you *sure* these people are with people they *should* be with?" But most simply accepted the information at face value. Soon, items began appearing on society pages across the continent.

Most guests were pleased with the results, but for at least one couple, Cash's publicity efforts proved to be a disaster.

Ralph Wilby was a gifted accountant and an adept embezzler. A Canadian, he had done most of his embezzling in the United States under an assumed name. From 1941 to 1943, as chief accountant for a New York management company, he managed to squirrel away $386,921. In January 1944, he informed his employer, who knew him as Alexander Hume, that he was going to Canada for a skiing vacation. Instead, Wilby and his third wife, Hazel, did a bunk. They made a leisurely trip across the country and checked into the Empress Hotel, signing the register "Mr. and Mrs. Ralph M. Wilby, Hamilton, Ontario."

Irving Strickland, a photographer with the *Victoria Times*, picked Hazel out of the crowd in the lobby. Hazel was the kind of girl it was hard to miss. "She had a physique that gave her distinction. She attracted attention wherever she went." Strickland let out a low whistle and went to the front desk. "Who is that pretty girl?" he asked. The desk clerk, aware of Gwen Cash's publicity-garnering technique, swung the register toward him. The following day, the *Times* ran a story mentioning "the beautiful Mrs. Ralph Wilby of Hamilton" who was visiting the Empress Hotel with her husband. A few days later, the item was picked up by newspapers in Hamilton and Toronto.

By now, Wilby's theft and his true identity had been discovered. A detective in Toronto spotted the story and informed the Victoria police. A contingent of the local constabulary marched down to the Empress Hotel and arrested him.

Wilby threw himself on the mercy of the court, admitting his guilt and returning most of the stolen money. Sentenced to Sing Sing, he would have been released no later than 1952, and he might well have returned to the Empress. Not because he had fond memories of the hotel, but because he had, according to Hazel, buried the missing $85,000 "along a highway near Victoria."

## Chapter Five

# A STATE OF MIND

**I**N THE SUMMER OF 1939, Agnes Newton Keith, who later recalled her wartime experiences in her book *Three Came Home*, was in Victoria with her husband, Harry, enjoying his "long leave" from his government job in British North Borneo. On 3 September, when Britain, and then Canada, declared war on Germany, Harry was ordered to return to Borneo immediately. As they waited in Victoria for their departure on the *Empress of Russia*, they witnessed a city being transformed.

"Every war has its tune, a song to make forever sad the hearts of those who have listened," Agnes remembered. " 'Roll Out the Barrel' was the enlistment tune in Victoria, played by the Canadian Scottish on every street corner. It followed us everywhere—into the Canadian Pacific steamship office, into the telegraph office, standing on the streets looking up to read the news bulletins above our heads, news which made our hearts stand still."

Within two weeks of the outbreak of war, seventeen members of the Empress Hotel staff had joined up. Harry Warburton, the assistant accountant and a veteran of the Great War, was serving as a regimental quartermaster-sergeant with the 1st Battalion Canadian Scottish. Head painter John Robertson, also a veteran of the first war, was a sergeant-major in the same regiment. Bellboy Fred Crewe joined the signalling corps; the bell captain, Tom Wilson, was with the ordnance corps; two members of the kitchen staff joined the air force.

Lady Mary Emily Swettenham moved into the Empress during the Second World War and remained a resident until her death some ten years later. This photograph was taken when she was presented at Buckingham Palace to King Edward VII and Queen Alexandra shortly after her marriage to Sir Alexander Swettenham, Governor of Jamaica.

*"There'll always be an England" was the theme of the 1940 Policemen's Ball in the Empress's Crystal Ballroom.*
COURTESY J. STRICKLAND

For some of the Empress's permanent guests, it was as if members of their families had been called to arms. Elevator boy Barney Lane had joined the Scottish before the war began. When his regiment was about to leave for overseas, he was invited to tea by Florence ffrench. "It was kind of uncomfortable. We were both on our best behaviour," Barney remembered. "But she did it again, six years later, when I came home."

At first it seemed as if the Empress would fare as badly in the Second World War as it had in the First. Once again, *Empress* liners were requisitioned for war work. But, by 1939, the hotel was relying less on the first-class passengers of the *Empress* line and more on Canadians and Americans.

After the Canadian government introduced restrictions which permitted travel outside the country only for business purposes, and even then limited spending to five dollars a day, residents of Manitoba, Ontario and Quebec could no longer escape to Florida for a break from winter and the Empress began to benefit from the CPR's promotion of Victoria as Canada's "Evergreen Playground." Americans, once again deterred from travelling to England by a European war, began to arrive in even greater numbers. As CPR promotions were careful to point out, "Canada Welcomes U.S. Citizens ... No Passports!"

But the most surprising development was the Empress's role as a "funk hole" for "fashionable refugees."

"Escapees poured in," Gwen Cash remembered. "Titled and untitled, they came from Europe, from the Orient and England itself."

Major General Sir James Drummond Graham and Lady Graham had been enjoying retirement on the Riviera when war broke out. They escaped from France and made their way to the Empress, where they settled in "for the duration." Stella and Asgar Petersen got out of Danzig in August 1939. The following summer, with her husband on active service with the British forces in Iceland, Stella drove across Canada to take refuge in the Empress. Sixty-six-year-old Lady Mary Emily Swettenham, the widow of Sir Alexander Swettenham, a former governor of Jamaica, arrived with her collection of antique tapestries, her diamonds, rubies, pearls and emeralds, her Spode dessert service, and crate-loads of her favourite furniture.

The Empress also welcomed domestic refugees. Wallace McMillan and his wife had retired to Victoria from Winnipeg a few years earlier. "We had a nice house in Victoria," Mrs. McMillan said, "but our gardener found he could make more money at the shipyard. Our maid left to get married. We thought the sensible thing to do was to move here." Especially so since the hotel's rate for long-term stays had fallen to $105 a month, half of what it had been a decade earlier.

Victoria became a military town. The Esquimalt Naval Base expanded. RCAF and RAF training bases were established at Patricia Bay. Hatley Park, the Dunsmuir family's great estate, became a military college. In Esquimalt, Yarrows shipyards worked around the clock producing ships for the navy.

It became something of a patriotic duty to attend the Empress's Christmas celebrations:

When on the evening of Dec. 25, carollers, clad in the velvets and silks, the pearl embroidered stomachers and stiff ruffs of Elizabethan days, march through the great hall of the

Empress hotel at Victoria to the sound of silver trumpets to "fire" the yule-log with all traditional pomp, they are in a sense proclaiming the Englishness of England; the continuance of her customs.

When the boar's head is carried aloft through the dining halls to the sound of song, it isn't just a domestic pig fixed up in the hotel kitchen to look like a tusked boar. It's the history of English ways. The story of the English people.

For "THERE'LL ALWAYS BE AN ENGLAND," and English customs, myths, and ideals outlive the centuries.

Christmas 1940 attracted nine hundred guests. Uniforms blended with formal dress. Canadians from the prairies, Montreal and Toronto, and Americans from New York, Los Angeles, Portland and Seattle rubbed shoulders with refugees from London, Paris, Oslo, Prague and the Riviera, and from Shanghai, Singapore and Hong Kong.

"It was," a guest remembered, "a remarkable assemblage."

By 1941, Victoria was a city at war. "One man out of four is in uniform," a visitor from San Francisco observed. "Each shop window is pasted with a 'V for Victory' and holds a poster urging you to 'Scuttle Hitler' by buying war savings bonds. Tourists receive a polite little brochure explaining where not to take pictures, and you are very careful not to ask if there are any British warships in the harbor."

On the morning of 22 May 1941, guests woke up to find a notice slipped under their doors. Beginning at ten o'clock that evening, blackout restrictions would be rehearsed. "Every Room in the Hotel MUST be completely darkened so that no lights of any kind are visible from the outside during the fifteen minute Blackout," the notice read. "Besides pulling the window blinds in bedroom and bathroom down fully, all lights MUST also be switched off. This is a Wartime Defence of Canada Order and anyone infringing the order is liable to heavy penalty."

That rattled a few nerves. But it was only a drill, only a precaution. The Empress Hotel continued to be regarded as a very safe place to sit out the war—until December 1941 when the Japanese attacked Pearl Harbor.

TOP *A wartime blackout practice notice.* EMPRESS HOTEL ARCHIVES

BOTTOM *Gas rationing during the Second World War took Empress guests back to the days when everyone arrived at the hotel by horse-drawn carriage rather than by car.* CANADIAN PACIFIC ARCHIVES

*An advertisement for the
Empress's traditional Winter
Golf Tournament.* CANADIAN
PACIFIC ARCHIVES A6534

**BLACK-OUT**

In view of present war conditions and the possibility of
black-out restrictions being enforced at any time during the night,
the Department of National Defence requests your co-operation in
seeing that all bedroom and bathroom lights are immediately exting-
uished once the Air Raid Siren is given . . . window shades completely
drawn down and side drapes pulled across the windows.

As air raid warning might be sounded while guests are
out of their bedroom, please see that all lights are ALWAYS ex-
tinguished, both in bathroom and bedroom, BEFORE LEAVING
YOUR ROOM.

In the event of an AIR RAID, guests are requested to
leave their rooms . . . without panic . . . and proceed DOWN THE
STAIRS to the Front Office, where they will be directed to Air Raid
Rooms located in Private Dining Rooms.

*After the attack on Pearl
Harbor, the private dining
rooms in the hotel's basement
were converted into air-raid
shelters and blackout notices
were posted in all Empress
bedrooms.* CANADIAN PACIFIC
ARCHIVES

Suddenly, the Pacific Coast seemed to be on the front line. A naval commander living in Esquimalt told his wife, "Don't bother planting those shrubs you ordered. The Japanese will be here before they bloom." An American friend wrote to Gwen Cash, "We particularly fear an attack from Alaska. It is supposed they will make a Pearl Harbor of Victoria and use British Columbia for a base to attack us."

Hong Kong fell on Christmas Day, Singapore in February. The possibility of an attack on Vancouver Island, and particularly on the capital city and on Esquimalt with its naval base and shipyard, began to seem very real. Gas rationing was introduced. The *Princess* steamers sailed under blackout restrictions. The provincial government began to make plans to send its library east of the Rockies.

The Department of Munitions and Supply began to organize for a Dunkirk-like evacuation of Vancouver Island. Fish boats, motor boats and sailboats with auxiliary engines were organized into squadrons and given the job of patrolling the coast and holding themselves "in a constant state of readiness" should an evacuation be ordered.

In spite of the rising panic, the Winter Golf Tournament took place as usual. Established in 1928 to lure off-season visitors to "balmy" Victoria and quickly dubbed the "Duffer's Delight" because everyone who entered won a prize, the tournament was sponsored by the Empress Hotel. The CPR promoted the event extensively and the Empress reduced its room rate by fifty cents a day, from $6.50 a day for a double room with bath to $42.00 for the same room for the full week of the tournament.

Attendance at the 14th Annual Tournament in March 1942 was good, but for some golfers, participation was a guilty pleasure. One woman described it as "a war work interlude"; another pointed out that she had knitting needles and wool stowed in her golf bag, ready to be put to work while she waited for her turn to tee off.

Travel restrictions had boosted attendance at the golf tournament by encouraging the participation of Canadians, but another government regulation led to the cancellation of the Garden Festival. On 20 March 1942, Gwen Cash reluctantly issued a press release. "Because of the new Canadian gas-rationing regulations which prohibit the use of sight-seeing buses, Victoria is compelled to cancel the Annual Spring Garden Festival."

On 7 June 1942 a Japanese submarine was reported to have sunk an American merchantman off Neah Bay. Less than a week later, the *Colonist* went to press with a banner headline, JAPANESE LAND ON ALEUTIAN ISLANDS. Then, on 20 June, news reached Victoria that the Estevan Point lighthouse on the west coast of the island had been fired upon by two enemy submarines, and a Vancouver newspaper warned that a Japanese invasion was "quite possible."

A retired general, who was now a member of the Canadian Senate and who was staying at the hotel during his tour of inspection of west coast fortifications, did his best to alarm the Empress dowagers. "He gallops up to old ladies staying at the hotel and asks them, 'What are you doing here? Why don't you go east of the Mountains where you belong? The military doesn't want you here!'"

Gwen Cash was reduced to a state of near-panic. "The Island is in danger," she confided to her journal. "Its vast forests can be fired this summer by incendiary bombs. And if not this summer, then next."

*The Dining Room framed a stunning view of the* Princess *boats at the CPR marine terminal. Crisp linen and heavy silver were part of the hotel's everyday service.* FROM A CPR BOOKLET, COURTESY J. CRYSLER

Blackout notices were posted in Empress guest rooms, and to prevent any chink of light escaping onto the harbour, a chain was strung across the steps to the Government Street entrance and the brass-bound revolving door was bolted shut.

But as weeks passed with no new emergencies, tensions eased. The revolving door was unlocked, and Empress guests settled into quiet routines. They learned not to grumble when the dinner menu, printed daily, informed them that, due to rationing, this would be another "meatless day"; and they became accustomed to dealing with a hotel full of uniforms.

Many servicemen and women were introduced to Empress-style gracious living while they were posted in Victoria. For Lois Duggan, who was sent to Victoria with the Wrens in 1943, the most enduring image of the city would be Florence ffrench gliding up to the porte-cochère in her electric car, one of the few cars still on the road since the advent of gas rationing.

The Empress Dining Room maintained a standard few young servicemen and women had experienced. Maître d'hôtel Jim Kemp was scrupulous in applying the CPR's *Manual of Service Rules*.

The manual, which included twenty pages of rules for waiters, put a great deal of stress on appearance:

> A waiter should take pride in his personal appearance. A well-groomed waiter is a credit to the house and wins the favor of patrons. Nothing is more repellant or offensive than an untidy waiter serving a guest. Not only the waiter's clothes, but his linen and his hands, finger nails, shoes and hair must be faultlessly clean and attended to. Hair should be closely trimmed. Black laced shoes with rubber heels should be worn at all times. He should always wash his hands before going on duty.

Every evening, before the Dining Room opened, Kemp required all the waiters to line up for inspection. As they stood to attention, their white gloves in their hands, he passed slowly down the line, checking the crease in their trousers and the shine on their shoes, pausing to examine the hands and fingernails of each man, and then waiting while they put on their gloves for a second inspection, palms up, palms down.

"It was just so professional, the dining-room service. You would just never hear a thing. No clash of china on china; no chink of silverware on dishes. It was seamless, soundless—professional."

Empress dining could be intimidating. The most basic table setting described by the *Manual* included thirteen items:

> 1 table napkin;
> 1 standard water goblet;
> 1 eight-inch bread and butter plate;
> 1 sugar bowl (for soft sugar);
> 1 sugar bowl (for lump sugar);
> 1 pair sugar tongs;
> 1 sugar spoon;
> 1 large silver-handled knife;
> 1 small silver-handled knife;

1 large silver fork;

1 small silver fork;

1 silver-top salt shaker;

1 silver-top pepper shaker.

One Victoria girl, invited to the Empress Dining Room by three airmen, "real prairie farm boys," found herself staring down at a dizzying array of silverware, carefully arranged on heavy white linen. Trying to decide which utensil to use, she dimly recalled the instruction to start on the outside and work in. As she reached, tentatively, for a fork, she looked up to find three pairs of eyes riveted on her hands. "They were all waiting for me, but I didn't really know what to do either."

Another Victoria girl met an American naval officer who was determined to have dinner in the hotel's Dining Room. "He had heard so much about it, but it was very crowded during the war. We were told that we might have a certain table, provided we left it before 8 P.M. One of the resident dowagers had had that same table for twenty years and nothing, but nothing, must disturb this routine."

In April 1943, the *Colonist* carried the report of "an Airman from Montreal" who had spent his six-day leave at the hotel:

Mornings were spent in the beautiful gardens of the hotel, the shouts of the children, swimming across the road in the Crystal Garden pool, was the only sound which interrupted the quietness and peacefulness of the morning, and as I sat back in my deck chair basking in the sun I wondered how it were ever possible for a war to be raging, such was the city's beauty and serenity.

He spent the rest of his time bicycling through Beacon Hill Park, roller-skating at the arena and listening to Billy Tickle entertain in the Lounge. All in all, a holiday of such outstanding rectitude that one suspects the "airman's" report originated at the desk of the hotel's press officer.

Other servicemen who visited the hotel had less innocent pleasures in mind. To insure that they caused the least possible disruption, the Empress instituted the practice of booking them into rooms on the first floor of the Humboldt wing, where they would be a safe remove from any of the regular guests and where there was nothing below them but salesmen's sample rooms. "Alcohol Alley" or "Drunkards' Alley" became so identified with men in uniform that desk clerks could not imagine sending them anywhere else, as one RAF officer discovered when he went to make arrangements for a room in which he and his bride could change after their wedding reception. "They were going to fire me down 'Drunkard's Alley,'" he recalled. "I said, 'No! You can't do that this time!'"

With so many servicemen stationed in and around Victoria, the city became the scene of hundreds of wartime weddings. "Brides, many accompanied by their parents, arrive by practically every boat to marry with the navy, the army, the air force." The social pages often reported as many as twenty-five weddings over a single weekend.

"The Empress should change its name to Honeymoon House," one resident quipped.

*The Billy Tickle Trio was a fixture in the Empress Lounge from 1928 until he retired in 1960.* EMPRESS HOTEL ARCHIVES

The Empress benefited from the war in another, rather unexpected, way when it became a focus for wartime filmmaking. The hotel was accustomed to entertaining Hollywood celebrities: during the 1930s, Rita Hayworth, Jack Benny, Pat O'Brien, Douglas Fairbanks, Katherine Hepburn, Bob Hope, Bing Crosby, Tallulah Bankhead and a host of others had passed through its lobby. Ginger Rogers had been pursued through the Lounge by a horde of adoring bobbysoxers. And Shirley Temple had arrived accompanied by her parents, amid rumours that she had fled from California because of kidnapping threats, a story that seemed to be borne out by the two huge bodyguards who took the room opposite hers and who always left their door open. The Empress had even, on one occasion, appeared in a Hollywood picture when Valerie Hobson was filmed getting married in the Grill Room for the feature *Tugboat Princess*.

But that was nothing compared to what happened in 1942, when Hollywood decided to take advantage of the fact that a film shot in Victoria could qualify as "British" and therefore avoid the tight quota system imposed by Britain on American films. War films had become a popular form of entertainment, and Hollywood producers discovered that southern Vancouver Island could masquerade as one particular European theatre of war—the forests and fiords of Norway.

In the spring of 1942, actor Paul Muni was signed to star as Erik Toresen, "a simple Norwegian fisherman who finds his quiet coastal village shattered by the Nazi invasion," in a film entitled *Commandos Come at Dawn*. (The title was not, in 1942, as risible as it would later become. However, the film was renamed *Commandos Strike at Dawn* before it was released.)

The cast included Lillian Gish, Sir Cedric Hardwicke, Robert Coote and Anna Lee. And quite a number of Victorians, including at least one member of the Empress staff, all of whom played Norwegian villagers, "untrained in the ways of war who use only their cold, sullen hatred as defense."

*Commandos Come at Dawn* promised to be a blockbuster. Based on a story by C. S. Forester, whose books included *Captain Horatio Hornblower* and *The African Queen*, and with a screenplay by Irwin Shaw, it was directed by John Farrow, who was rumoured to have a million-dollar budget at his disposal.

The director, the cast and all the members of the crew stayed at the Empress. But more than that, all the rooms on the hotel's lower floor—the Georgian Lounge and the private dining rooms—were converted into the art department and the prop department. In one room, two local architects, Douglas James and Hubert Savage, produced construction drawings for the Norwegian village that was built on Finlayson Arm near Bamberton. In another room, the hotel's painters worked on backdrops for the interior scenes which would be filmed in one of the exhibition buildings at the Willows Fairground.

On 16 July, Paul Muni checked into a suite in the Humboldt wing, looked admiringly about him and endeared himself to the management by declaring, "This is really beautiful. I have never seen anything like it, even in the finest hotels in New York."

He then settled down to become one of the coldest, most aloof celebrity guests the staff had ever encountered. "He was always complaining," a desk clerk remembered. "He got really mad when the whistle of the midnight boat blasted him awake every night."

As an action hero, Muni left something to be desired. "He didn't like having to scramble

TOP *In 1946, the Lounge featured theatre lobby-style carpets. The "guests" are actually members of the staff dressed in their best.* CANADIAN PACIFIC ARCHIVES

BOTTOM *Room 278 was one of the larger rooms on the second floor of the centre block facing the harbour. By the mid-1940s even the better rooms seemed homey rather than grand. (See colour photo 19.)* EMPRESS HOTEL ARCHIVES M3630

around in the bracken. Thought he might scratch his hands. They had to get him flesh-coloured gloves to wear," a porter scoffed.

There was secret rejoicing when some of the "commandos" came off second best during a run-in with the indomitable Billy Tickle. Born in 1895, William Fletcher Tickle was a short, round, jaunty little man. He had begun his career playing violin in the orchestra pit of the Capital Theatre, providing musical accompaniment for silent films. In 1928, he had joined the Empress as the hotel's musical director. By 1942, the Billy Tickle Trio—Billy on violin, Malcolm More on piano and cellist Frank Balagno—had become an Empress institution. Every evening at six o'clock, they took up their position in the Lounge by the open Dining Room door, and played until ten when the Dining Room closed.

Tickle was famous for his memory. A guest who had requested a particular song on his last visit would be greeted by the same tune when he returned. He was equally famous for his insistence on doing things the proper way. To guests who complained when he played a shortened version of "God Save the King" at the end of the evening, he would patiently explain that, according to protocol, only the first six bars should be played, unless the sovereign was actually present.

One evening, some American members of the *Commandos'* crew who had done some serious

drinking in their rooms before coming down to dinner, asked Tickle to play "The Star Spangled Banner." Tickle stoutly refused; a dozen people stormed out. "But one simply *does not* play the anthems of foreign countries," Tickle explained.

Two years later, during the filming of another motion picture, the Empress witnessed an incident that was a good deal more unpleasant. In 1944, Vancouver Island was once again asked to pose as the coast of Norway for the MGM feature *Son of Lassie*. Described as "the heartwarming sequel to *Lassie Come Home*," the film was the unlikely story of a young RAF navigator forced to parachute out of his bomber over enemy territory with his dog, Laddie, in his arms. Nigel Bruce and Donald Crisp reprised their roles in the original film, and Peter Lawford was cast as a grown-up Roddy McDowall.

A few days before filming was about to commence, the real star of the film arrived in Victoria with his trainer, Rudd Weatherwax. Lassie met the press on the front lawn of the Empress Hotel and performed some tricks, attracting an admiring crowd and earning wide coverage in local newspapers. Peter Lawford's arrival in Victoria was not considered a matter of great moment. However, his departure from the Empress Hotel would become a staff legend.

Lassie and Weatherwax booked into a small apartment hotel with an enclosed private garden. The rest of the cast and crew checked into the Empress. Lawford was twenty-one years old, deliciously handsome and not at all happy. Although it was August, the weather was windy and cool. Unfortunately for Lawford, the scene in which he and Lassie were called upon to swim to a rocky shore after having escaped their Nazi pursuers was filmed at Christopher Point, in the frigid waters of the Strait of Juan de Fuca.

"Both Lassie and Peter Lawford were equally reluctant to plunge into the icy water," an observer noted. Lassie ruined the first take by shaking vigorously as soon as the two clambered out of the water. On the second take, Lassie got it right. "The dog scrambled up with Mr. Weatherwax shouting instructions at him. Lawford clawed at the rock as if exhausted, stripped off his coat, wrapped it around Lassie and hugged the dog, as the director called 'Cut.' "

Lassie was immediately wrapped in blankets and taken back to town to dry off and warm up. Lawford peeled off his soaking sweater, pulled off his sodden boots, then ran barefoot over rocks and thistles toward dry clothes.

"The dog had a dressing room, but I didn't," he grumbled. "Lassie was insured for a million, and I had the suspicion that if I was insured at all, it was for a substantially smaller amount."

Lawford spent his evenings nursing his wounded pride, and the cuts and bruises of each day's shoot, with a few stiff drinks. Room-service waiter Peter Shippen recalled one particular night:

> We got a call from Lawford's suite for ice and mixer. It was August; the hotel was busy. No waiters were available. Normally, we never asked women to act as room-service waiters, but we thought 'Well, ice and mixer isn't heavy. Let's send Rita.'
>
> Rita was fifteen or sixteen; she usually worked as a bus girl, but when it was very busy, she was pressed into room service. She went up to Lawford's room; she was walking to the table with her tray when he slammed the door behind her, locked it and threw her on the

bed. She screamed and *screamed*. The hotel detective burst in. Lawford was told to pack his bags and then he, and his luggage, were escorted to the street.

And Peter Lawford entered Empress myth as "the only celebrity to ever be thrown, bodily, out of the hotel."

In one way or another, the Empress Hotel did very well out of the war. In 1943, the hotel rolled up a profit of $150,000, the highest achieved since 1913. Profits doubled the following year, but the CPR had a nagging worry; the city's concessions were about to expire.

Since 1925, the hotel had been paying a flat tax of $10,000 a year. If no further concessions were granted, the tax bill would rise to over $54,000 in 1945. The CPR trotted out the usual arguments and asked that the existing flat rate be extended for an additional twenty years. After several tough negotiating sessions, an agreement with the city was worked out. All the concessions enjoyed by the Crystal Garden would continue for an additional twenty years. The Empress would lose its special status regarding water rates, but taxes would be fixed at $34,000 for twenty years.

Four times Victorians had been called to the polls to ratify agreements between the city and the CPR, and four times they had shown their appreciation for the company's efforts on the city's behalf. The fifth vote, on 26 June 1944, produced a similar result, with 1,184 favouring the proposal while only 208 were opposed.

In 1945, the hotel posted a profit of $410,000, the highest in its thirty-seven-year history. But with the end of the war, the Empress's income began a steady decline. As only one of the four Pacific *Empresses* had survived the war, the CPR decided to abandon the service and concentrate instead on air travel. But although Canadian Pacific Airlines would institute a trans-Pacific route, the planes would not be touching down in Victoria. The ships of the CPR's aging *Princess* fleet, which were capable of carrying only a few cars, began to suffer from the growing trend toward private automobile ownership. And with travellers demanding speed rather than comfort, the popularity of the midnight sailings began to decline. In 1948, the night service between Victoria and Seattle was cancelled, and the Victoria-Vancouver midnight boat would be discontinued eleven years later.

Since the hotel's books were sliding into the red, the CPR had very little enthusiasm for spending money on upgrading or improvements. And perhaps that was just as well. Until the 1960s (by which time things had gone rather too far), the hotel's aura of genteel decay—its refusal to succumb to modernity, its old-fashioned quaintness—was an essential ingredient in its charm.

"The Empress isn't a hotel," a resident explained. "It's a state of mind."

♔

_Chapter Six_

# THE ESSENCE OF VICTORIA

I N DECEMBER 1950, IN A FEATURE ARTICLE for _Maclean's_ magazine, titled "The Eccentric Empress of Victoria," Bruce Hutchison defined the hotel's special character.

"The Empress was designed as a resort for strangers. Its chief product, unforseen by the designers, is purely Victorian. By its complex chemistry of men, scenery, architecture, horticulture and illusion it has distilled, bottled and preserved the inner essence of Victoria."

Part of Victoria's "inner essence" was its calm acceptance of odd behaviour—provided, of course, that the oddness was of the quaintly eccentric, British variety. And like the city, the Empress suffered eccentrics gladly.

John Rowland had been a "lobby-sitter" for as long as anyone could remember. A "kindly old gentleman," he lived on a small pension in a rooming house at the corner of Government and Belleville Streets where he cooked on a hot plate under the light of a single naked bulb.

"He was one of the city's lovable characters," a newspaperman recalled. "You weren't a Victorian unless you knew John Rowland, either by name, by sight or both." During the day, he might be spotted taking his constitutional along the Causeway; sitting, fast asleep, in the public gallery of the legislature; catching forty winks on a park bench; or sitting at a lunch counter, making one cup of coffee last the afternoon. But there was one place that he could always be found. Every night from six o'clock

♔

until ten, he was in the Lounge of the Empress Hotel.

For thirty years, ever since the end of the Great War when he had come to Victoria to live on his soldier's pension, he had assumed his position in the Lounge—always in a comfortable armchair beside the grandfather clock. As the years passed, he became shabbier and shabbier. He took to wearing two threadbare coats, and there were often egg stains on his tie. But his courtliness remained unchanged. Approached by a hotel guest, he would stand and bow before extending his hand and exchanging the pleasantries of the day.

Like Rowland himself, his chair became shabby and worn. "That chair got really disgusting," the assistant manager said. "We hid it under a slipcover during the day and whisked it off just before John arrived."

He became a hotel fixture, a great favourite with returning guests. Post cards and letters and Christmas cards arrived, from all over the world, addressed simply to "John Rowland, By the Grandfather Clock, Empress Hotel."

Rowland was a music lover—Billy Tickle's most devoted fan and a composer in his own right, having written the words and music to "British Columbia." The music was in a march tempo, and the lyrics were heartfelt rather than stirring:

> There's a land out west you'll love to see
> Where song birds sing merrily
> Where the scenes are pretty as can be
> In British Columbia

In 1939 Rowland had somehow managed to find the money to copyright "British Columbia," and over the years he had paid for the printing of hundreds of copies—all of which he autographed with a flourish and gave away. "He was spending money on that song when he should have been buying ham sandwiches for himself," a friend said. Billy Tickle often included "British Columbia" in his evening repertoire, but the happiest day of Rowland's life came in 1951 when Princess Elizabeth and the Duke of Edinburgh dined at the hotel as guests of the government. "Tickle placed John's song right at the top of the program," an acquaintance recalled. "A graceful compliment to shabby old John Rowland." The composer died only a month later.

John Rowland had never spent a dime in the Empress, but, as manager Kirk Hodges said, "He was one of our characters—he was a nice old fellow—he loved music and he loved people. Why shouldn't he have sat in our lounge every night?"

But then, Hodges was not without his own behavioural quirk. Every morning, as soon as the hotel's print shop had produced that day's menu, page-boy Jack Ellett was instructed to take it directly to the manager's office. Hodges carefully studied the menu and then made his selection of the meal that would later be served to his pet Pekinese.

Joseph Zanichelli, who replaced Jim Kemp as maître d'hôtel in 1951, demonstrated the same quiet acceptance of eccentricity. Born in Tuscany and having learned his trade in hotel kitchens in France and Italy and as a dining-room steward on French Line ships sailing between Cherbourg and New York, he brought to his job a European suavity and flair, combined with unerring discretion and tact.

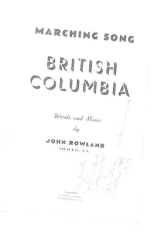

MARCHING SONG
BRITISH COLUMBIA
Words and Music by
JOHN ROWLAND

TOP *John Rowland, photographed in 1950, was a fixture in the Empress Hotel's lobby for upwards of thirty years.*
PRIVATE COLLECTION

BOTTOM *In 1947, John Rowland presented an autographed copy of the song he wrote, "British Columbia," to page-boy John Steeves.*
COURTESY J. STEEVES

One of the Empress's regular guests was an old colonel who checked into the hotel several times a year, carrying with him boxes of lead soldiers. He had his own private supply of a hard-to-get brand of gin, which Zanichelli stored in his office between the old soldier's visits. For three or four days, the colonel would shut the door to his room, get royally drunk and refight long-ago battles with his toy soldiers. Zanichelli made sure that the colonel was kept supplied with gin, personally carried his meals to his room and kept an eye on him until he checked out, refreshed, a few days later.

Zanichelli himself had a rather odd avocation. He liked octopus. He liked to catch it and he liked to eat it. "His favourite hobby was to go down to the shore, past the Parliament Buildings," a friend recalled. "He'd take a can of carbide in a cheesecloth bag, stick it under the rocks, and bring up the biggest octopus you've ever seen."

The management's policy of taking unusual behaviour as a matter of course included the permanent residents. One retired couple, who lived for years in two fifth-floor rooms overlooking the garden, ordered their dinner from room service every night. And always the same meal—black Alaska cod, a boiled potato and peas. "Every night!," an assistant manager exclaimed. "For years! Easter! Thanksgiving! Even for Christmas!"

Another couple had similarly regular habits. Every evening, they dined at 6:15. Afterwards, they moved to the Lounge and occupied a chesterfield to which they considered themselves as having exclusive rights. He sat in one corner and she sat in the other. They read until Billy Tickle played "The King" and then retired to their room without having exchanged a word the entire evening.

The hotel's gentlemen residents were also creatures of habit. One man came down from his room every evening at 7:30 and took a seat close to the orchestra. For ten minutes he would read his newspaper, then go to sleep. Promptly at 8:30 he would wake up and proceed upstairs to his room. Another guest, who had moved into the Humboldt wing almost as soon as it opened, rose every morning at seven and walked all around the hotel grounds, picking up little pieces of litter with his cane.

Lady Swettenham, who had taken up residence in a fourth-floor room in 1942, was a fixture at the Empress and a mainstay of Victoria society. When attending functions at Government House, she made it a habit to wear her magnificent stomacher, a stiff, diamond-encrusted panel, laced over the bodice-front of her dress. "It always caused a stir," a society matron said. "It was one of the few stomachers left in North America."

Most of Lady Swettenham's clothes dated from the days before the Great War when she had been the chatelaine of Government House in Jamaica. Even after arthritis forced her to hobble about on two sticks, she remained a distinguished figure in the Empress Lounge, clad in satin, laden with jewels and with one of her prized possessions, a sweeping black Chantilly lace shawl, draped over her shoulders.

Like many of the Empress dowagers, Lady Swettenham was concerned about her finances. Charity bazaars became familiar with her traditional donation—carefully gift-wrapped tiny bars of soap imprinted with the words "Empress Hotel." She really need not have worried. When she died in 1953, she left $74,000; enough, at the time, to be described as a large estate.

Florence ffrench, too, worried that she would outlive her fortune. After Dr. ffrench died in 1951 in his eightieth year, his widow stayed on at the Empress. She became so thin and frail that staff members became alarmed. "She was a lovely old girl," a maid remembered. "We felt sorry for her because she looked so hard up, as if she never got enough to eat. We used to save her things, take her chocolates to perk her up." Florence died in 1962. She had been living at the hotel for forty-two years—the longest tenure of any permanent resident. To the staff members who had worried about her, it came as something of a surprise when the probate of her will revealed an estate of $245,000.

Leah Rogers was quite the opposite. With her husband, Charles, she had built up a world-famous candy business, the name Rogers Chocolate becoming known far and wide. The Rogers had started their Government Street store soon after their marriage in 1888. After their fifteen-

*The Empress's first cocktail lounge, the Coronet Room, opened in 1954 in the former Reading Room. Its most striking feature was the dark blue carpet, designed specially for the Empress and featuring coronets, Tudor roses and wreaths.*

B.C. ARCHIVES F-01924

year-old son committed suicide in 1905, their business became their obsession. They poured money into a new store, with ornate fittings and heavy bevelled glass, while they continued to live in a little James Bay house without electricity or indoor plumbing. They started work at four in the morning, and often, during the winter, spent the night at the store, sleeping in rocking chairs pulled up to the big stove. When Charles Rogers died in 1927, his shop was valued at $19,230, his home at $3,900.

Leah Rogers was left a very wealthy widow; Charles's estate amounted to $295,985. She sold the candy store, moved into the Empress and set about giving her fortune away. By the time she died in 1952, she had succeeded. She had given up her room at the hotel and had been living in a nursing home on a small government pension. There was not enough money left to pay for adding her name to her husband's tombstone.

Hotel guests looked for their favourite lobby-fixtures on their return. "A lot of our guests will miss him," Kirk Hodges said after John Rowland's death. And several months after Lady Swettenham died, the *Colonist* reported: "Many annual summer visitors have missed her. They say the Empress lounge is not quite the same without her presence."

There was another breed of permanent resident about which visitors might not have developed the same fondness had they known about them. They were the cats who made their home in the sub-basement, in the bowels of the building. The only other occupants were the Chinese employees who used a corner of the sub-basement to sort through the dining-room slops in search of mistakenly discarded silver. Perhaps the cats managed to live on those slops, or perhaps they relied mostly on rats. Whatever the case, they thrived.

By the early forties, the sub-basement was populated by a whole colony of inbred, feral cats—cats who had never seen the light of day and who were glimpsed by members of the staff only when they ventured into the basement with a flashlight. "The light would catch their eyes. All those eyes staring back at you. My God, it was eerie."

While management might have only tolerated the cats, they had become positively indulgent about standards of private behaviour. The manager scarcely raised an eyebrow when a cabinet minister from Vancouver, who lived at the hotel when the legislature was in session, checked in with his mistress, and the two lived together "quite flagrantly." However, the hotel was "almost an extension of the legislature," and the politician's colleagues, fearing scandal, had a quiet word with the manager. The mistress returned to Vancouver, and the cabinet minister took to catching the midnight boat.

The minister's conduct had left the manager unruffled. But then, he was equally complacent about the prostitute who operated out of her room on the sixth floor.

She had been there for several years before it occurred to one of the other permanent residents that something unusual was going on. She brought her concerns to Ken Woodward, the assistant manager. He consulted with the manager.

"She ever make any trouble?" he demanded.

"No."

"Any other complaints?"

*Menu cover for the Royal dinner, 30 May 1939.*
COURTESY B. LANE

OPPOSITE *The Dining Room was arranged in an unusual configuration to accommodate the 250 guests invited to dine with King George VI and Queen Elizabeth on 30 May 1939.* COURTESY B. LANE

"No."

"Well, does she pay her bills on time?"

Yes, Woodward told him, always on time, always the full amount. The manager shrugged his shoulders. "Well then, I can't think that it's any of our business what she does up there."

During the early fifties, the hotel continued to struggle with British Columbia's strict liquor laws. When a dedicated teetotaller, W. A. C. Bennett, was elected premier in 1952 and celebrated with an "Ovaltine Party" at the Empress Hotel, the prospect for change did not look promising. But changing public taste and the pressure applied by the hotel and liquor industries proved impossible to resist. In April 1954, British Columbians voted to approve the sale of liquor by the glass.

The Empress Hotel received one of the first "dining lounge licences" issued by the provincial Liquor Control Board, and on 17 July 1954, the Dining Room began serving wine to the public for the first time in thirty-seven years. By August, when the Liquor Control Board issued a "lounge licence," the Empress was ready.

During the spring and summer, $85,000 had been spent to convert the Reading and Writing Room into a cocktail lounge, carefully designed to comply with liquor board regulations that prohibited "necking booths," required illumination "to a minimum of three foot-candles" and insisted on "well-spaced" tables and chairs, arranged to provide every customer with a full view of the entire room. A bartender was transferred from the company's Royal York Hotel in Toronto to instruct the staff; and when the Coronet Lounge opened for business in August, he had perfected the "Empress Special," a mixture of rye, pineapple juice and grenadine, served in a sugared cocktail glass.

"The manager thought the Coronet Room would just take off," Ken Woodward remembered. "The first night it was pretty well full, but after that the crowds got smaller and smaller. People who were used to buying their own bottle found the drinks just too expensive!"

But gradually, they became accustomed to the new regime. Six months later, a chambermaid was able to report that there was much less drinking in Empress bedrooms.

*King George VI and Queen Elizabeth leave the Empress Hotel accompanied by B.C. Premier "Duff" Patullo on 30 May 1939.*
B.C. ARCHIVES B-08114

In 1957, the Empress Hotel became the official vice-regal residence. On 15 April, British Columbia's Government House was destroyed by fire. Lieutenant-Governor Frank Ross and Mrs. Ross escaped in their nightclothes and took refuge in the Empress. For a time the government toyed with the idea of renting one of Victoria's grand homes as a temporary Government House, but in the end decided to install the Rosses in the vice-regal suite for an annual rent of $20,000.

The lieutenant-governor's flag remained flying from the Empress flagpole for a full two years until 1959, when a new Government House was ready. During those two years, the Empress welcomed the first member of the British Royal family to ever, officially, bed down in the hotel.

The Empress was no stranger to royalty. In 1919, Edward, Prince of Wales had waltzed into the dawn in the Crystal Ballroom—an event considered by Victorians to be of such importance that almost fifty years later, the obituaries of elderly ladies would appear under headlines such as "Mrs. Thornley-Hall Dies. Prince of Wales Singled Her Out."

Eight years later, Edward was back for an unofficial visit. On that occasion, while he was supposedly staying at Government House, he booked a five-room suite at the Empress. The hotel doorman, who was instructed to stay at his post every evening until the prince returned, found his shift stretching to 2:30 in the morning, when Edward swept up to the door in a taxi.

During the 1930s, two royal families were overnight guests. In 1931, King Prajadhipok of Siam, accompanied by his wife, Queen Rambi Barni, passed through the city on their way to and from Baltimore, where the King was to undergo an operation for cataracts, his chronic eye problems attributed to the fact that he took his self-appointed role as his country's film censor altogether too seriously.

He was a sad little man. Only thirty-eight years old, he suffered from recurrent bouts of malaria, and although he had ascended the throne of Siam six years earlier, his background was mostly English—he was educated at Eton and at the Royal Military Academy and served as a lieutenant in the Royal Horse Artillery during the Great War. Still, he was an absolute monarch, and he travelled in the appropriate style. He and his fifty-six-member entourage booked an entire floor of the Empress; porter Jimmy Phillips handled over five hundred pieces of luggage; and the hotel's cooks made way for the Siamese chefs who prepared the king's food.

Gwen Cash recalled another royal visit. "I remember seeing the little Japanese princess and her husband, Heir Apparent to the Imperial Throne of Japan, on their way back from the Coronation of George VI. She was not allowed to go shopping, although she wanted to, very badly. The Sino-Japanese war had recently broken out. The authorities were afraid something terrible might happen on Canadian soil."

*Assignment of rooms for the 1939 Royal tour.* PRIVATE COLLECTION

With Victoria still considering itself very much a part of the Empire, the highlight of the decade came in 1939, when King George VI and Queen Elizabeth came to lunch. Twelve years later, Princess Elizabeth visited the Empress, but, like her parents, she was there only for a government-hosted luncheon.

It was not until 1958 that a member of the British royal family became an acknowledged overnight guest. Princess Margaret was to visit British Columbia to help the province celebrate the hundredth anniversary of the formation of the Colony of British Columbia. As the time of her visit neared, an air of expectancy hovered over the hotel. The hallway leading to the vice-regal suite was repainted in a soft pink, and an Empress chef, overwhelmed at the thought of cooking for royalty, cut his finger so that he would be banished from the kitchen. But Margaret proved to be "a charming young lady" whose tastes were simple. Maître d'hôtel Joe Zanichelli noted:

She likes roast beef, sliced thin, sea-food, chicken, lamb, cheese (quite frequently her dessert was fruit and cheese), butter (she took two or three pieces at each meal), coffee and tea— she took two demi-tasses of coffee after each meal except breakfast, for breakfast she had her own tea. She dislikes champagne, melon, caviar, soups and consommes, souffles and puddings and potatoes. She eats comparatively little and she eats fairly rapidly.

The only anxious moments came on the night the princess decided to go up on the hotel's roof. The Russian satellite "Sputnik" was scheduled to pass over the city. Orbiting space hardware was still a novelty, and Margaret wanted to see it. The best vantage point was a rooftop platform used only by the staff members who raised and lowered the flags. It was reached by steep ladder-like stairs and protected by a flimsy railing.

"She can't go up there!" Ken Woodward gasped. But the manager, Cyril Chapman, said, "Well, I suppose we don't have any choice." A chair was hurriedly placed on the platform. Chapman and Woodward held their breath as the princess, Lieutenant-Governor and Mrs. Ross, and several members of the royal entourage made their way up the shaky stairs to the roof. "It was a dark windy night. We thought, 'My God, we might lose them all.'"

"Of course, it was a great honour to have Her Royal Highness here," Chapman said a few days later. "I suppose the publicity which has developed is worth millions."

During the 1950s, Hollywood royalty continued to call. Bob Hope and Bing Crosby were frequent guests, Hope chipping golf balls on the Empress lawn and Crosby so relaxed by the hotel's restful charm that he went without his toupee. When assistant manager Ken Woodward read in the Vancouver papers that Hope, Crosby and bandleader Phil Harris were staying at the Hotel Vancouver, he was not at all surprised to receive a call from their advance-man saying they were planning to visit the Empress. He explained the type of accommodation they would require—three adjoining suites—and told Woodward they would be arriving at two o'clock on Tuesday afternoon. On Monday, the advance-man arrived. He checked the rooms, gave further instructions and stayed at the hotel that night. The following morning, he told the desk clerk he was checking out, travelling to Seattle to make arrangements for their arrival at the Olympic Hotel.

"But," he said, "I'm a little short of money. Could you cash a cheque for me?" The desk clerk said, "Well, yes, I suppose we can. How much?" "Oh, make it $800," the advance-man smiled.

At two o'clock that afternoon, the manager, the assistant manager and a *Colonist* reporter were lined up at the hotel entrance. By ten past two, they began to get fidgety. At 2:30, the manager said, "We'd better call the Hotel Vancouver."

"They had been there, alright," Woodward said. "But they'd checked out days earlier and they certainly weren't coming here."

In February 1957, the manager estimated that the Empress had registered 5,400,000 guests since 1908. Approaching its fiftieth birthday, the hotel had become a world unto itself. A staff of four hundred worked in fourteen departments. During the summer season, the housekeeping department made a thousand beds every day and swept three miles of corridors. In the kitchen, a staff of forty-one prepared everything from scratch. Every day they baked 100 pies, 350 loaves of bread and more than 2,000 rolls. Over the year, they prepared 30 tons of meat, 50 tons of fowl, one-and-a-half tons of salmon and half a ton of crab. The hotel laundry coped with an annual load of almost six million pieces of linen, and the maintenance department counted on replacing 17,000 light bulbs a year.

*Luncheon
tendered by
Her Majesty's Government
of The Province of British Columbia
in honour of
Her Royal Highness
The Princess Margaret*

*Empress Hotel
Victoria, British Columbia
Monday, July fourteenth
nineteen hundred and fifty eight*

Menu cover for a luncheon held in honour of Princess Margaret in 1958.

PRIVATE COLLECTION

TOP *In 1951, Princess Elizabeth and the Duke of Edinburgh were guests of the government at a luncheon in the Empress Hotel. Standing behind the princess, looking rather worried, is maître d'hôtel Joe Zanachelli. Since becoming queen, Elizabeth has returned to the hotel on three other occasions.* CANADIAN PACIFIC ARCHIVES

BOTTOM *Princess Margaret, photographed leaving the Empress with Lieutenant-Governor and Mrs. Ross in 1958.* COURTESY J. RYAN

*Room 324 was on the third floor of the Humboldt wing.*
*The furniture was new in 1929. By 1946, it was becoming*
*rather tired.* CANADIAN PACIFIC ARCHIVES M3622

OPPOSITE *The Lounge in 1955 looked just the way it had ten years*
*earlier: the same carpets, the same furniture and the same feeling.*
COURTESY E. PENTY

The garden produced equally impressive statistics. A new head gardener, Art Sanders, was building on Fred Saunders's original plan. Every year, 125,000 plants were set out in beds around the hotel, including 3,000 begonias, 2,600 chrysanthemums and 3,000 brick-red geraniums, developed, Sanders liked to boast, from six cuttings taken from the gardens of Buckingham Palace. In addition, the gardens contained 3,500 wallflowers, 120 varieties of roses and 308 varieties of dahlias. Then there were the 600 carnations, grown as cut-flowers, and the 250,000 bulbs, including daffodils, hyacinths, snowdrops, tulips and crocuses.

In the Conservatory, the palms had reached 18 feet, the lemon tree planted in 1929 was producing fruit, and the orange tree was expected to begin bearing soon.

On paper, it seemed as though the Empress Hotel was thriving. But there was trouble afoot. Other than the money that had been spent converting the library into a cocktail lounge, no major capital investment had been made in the hotel since 1929.

In 1957, a visitor, described as a seasoned traveller, gave his impression of the Empress Hotel: "I ask you where else could you see such a place? Can you imagine it! I'm paying $22 a day for a suite in there. It's got a bathtub on legs, the beds are brown enamel. So much of it is old fashioned. I travel all over the world and never have I seen anything like it. It's all so different. But, boy, how I love the place. There's absolutely nothing like it, and I'm glad there's a place like it that I can come to and really feel at home."

Not all the Empress's guests would have agreed with him.

*Head gardener Art Sanders, photographed in the Empress's Conservatory in November 1946.*
B.C. ARCHIVES D-02707

# PORTFOLIO
## *Renovation and Restoration*

17. AND 18. *The Lounge (previous page) and the Dining Room as they appeared after Operation Teacup, the first major renovation undertaken in almost forty years. In keeping with the tenor of the times, Operation Teacup emphasized modernization rather than restoration.* EMPRESS HOTEL ARCHIVES

19. *In 1988, work began on the Royal Renovation, a multimillion-dollar programme designed to return the Empress to its former glory. The redecorated bedrooms, bright with fresh chintz, provided a level of comfort unknown in earlier years (see page 87).*

20. TOP *During the Royal Renovation, the Dining Room was divided in two. Focussed on the fireplace, part of the room retained its original function, while the harbourview end of the room became the Lobby Lounge.* CANADIAN PACIFIC ARCHIVES T05-72-89, MARIO MADAU PHOTO

21. BOTTOM *The Lobby Lounge, featuring dining room light fixtures from 1908, was designed as a comfortable, heritage-style cocktail lounge to replace the Library Bar, which was converted into retail space. (See page 83 for similar view in the 1930s.)* CANADIAN PACIFIC ARCHIVES T05-68-89, MARIO MADAU PHOTO

22. OPPOSITE *The Lounge was rechristened the Tea Lobby and furnished to provide the maximum comfort for guests partaking in afternoon tea— the Empress's most enduring tradition.* CANADIAN PACIFIC ARCHIVES T05-62-89, MARIO MADAU PHOTO

23. *The colours used in the restored Crystal Ballroom gave the room a warmth*
*and a feeling of opulence unknown in its earlier years.*

CANADIAN PACIFIC ARCHIVES T05-67-89, MARIO MADAU PHOTO

24. *The Bengal Room retained its Indian theme, enhanced by the addition of murals,*
*handpainted in France and "redolent of the Raj."*

CANADIAN PACIFIC ARCHIVES T05-72-89, MARIO MADAU PHOTO

25. OPPOSITE *The rebuilt Conservatory linked the Empress to the new conference centre, designed by architect Nicholas Bawlf to echo the Crystal Garden.* CANADIAN PACIFIC ARCHIVES

26. TOP *In the hotel's Lounge, the wall-to-wall carpeting was peeled back to reveal the original oak floor with its intricately patterned inlay, and a new colour scheme picked out formerly unnoticed details.* CANADIAN PACIFIC ARCHIVES T05-61-89

27. BOTTOM *With its new stained-glass dome and restored ceiling, the Palm Court re-emerged as one of the Empress's most beautiful public rooms.* CANADIAN PACIFIC ARCHIVES T0-64-89, MARIO MADAU PHOTO

28. *By 1997, the Tea Lobby was entertaining 100,000 guests a year for afternoon tea. (See colour photo 3 for a similar view almost ninety years earlier.)*

EMPRESS HOTEL ARCHIVES, JOHN SHERLOCK PHOTO

29. *Within ten years of the Royal Renovation, all the bedrooms and suites had been redone in richer, more vibrant hues.* EMPRESS HOTEL ARCHIVES

30. NEXT PAGE *As the Empress approached its ninetieth year, the gardens continued to play an important role in its charm.* EMPRESS HOTEL ARCHIVES, JOHN SHERLOCK PHOTO

# Part Three

# THE GRAND OLD LADY OF GOVERNMENT STREET

Until the mid-1960s, when the
hotel attempted to project a more
youthful image, the impression
most people had of the Empress
was of sedate quietude.
EMPRESS HOTEL ARCHIVES
21269

## Chapter Seven

# THINKING
# THE UNTHINKABLE

ON 20 JANUARY 1958, THE EMPRESS TURNED FIFTY—without fanfare but with "tea as usual."

"Sedate old ladies prefer to ignore their own birthdays. The Empress is no exception," the *Colonist* teased. But the newspaper had missed the real significance of the date. In exchange for over six acres of city land, the CPR had promised to open and keep operating a hotel for fifty years, and within that time to use none of the land for anything other than hotel purposes. The Empress had fulfilled that obligation. Now, the CPR owned the land free and clear. The company could do what it liked with the grounds and gardens. It could, in fact, sell, close or demolish the hotel.

Nothing suggested that the company should act in haste. The Empress, still operating as Government House, was expecting a number of distinguished guests during 1958, British Columbia's centennial year. In addition, visitors to the World's Fair, planned for 1962 in Seattle, were expected to make side trips to the city and generate untold profits for all Victoria hostelries. And, finally, the tax concessions which the CPR was receiving from the city would not expire until 1965. Any hard decisions about the future of the Empress could be postponed until then. But, in the meantime, there was no reason why the CPR should not attempt to winkle the maximum profit out of the hotel's gardens.

The Empress gardens had been laid out in a more leisurely era when travellers were met by the hotel's horse-drawn carriage as they disembarked from an *Empress* liner or a *Princess* steamer. But with

*In 1961, a bus depot was built at the corner of Douglas and*
*Belleville Streets, on the site formerly occupied by the hotel's tennis courts.*

more and more tourists arriving in the city by automobile, the Empress's manager, Cyril Chapman, decided that the hotel needed a car park. And besides, if he made it a "pay" parking lot, he could increase the hotel's revenues.

In February 1958, the CPR announced that an acre of the grounds, including the clay tennis courts, would be blacktopped to provide space for 150 cars. The company promised that the parking lot would be hidden by shrubbery and trellis work, but a row of fifty-year-old trees along the Douglas Street frontage could not be saved. "Desecration!" a Victoria alderman exploded.

There was worse to come. Three years later, in March 1961, the company revealed details of an agreement with Vancouver Island Coach Lines. The CPR would build and lease to the bus company a two-storey terminal to be constructed on the hotel's parking lot at the corner of Douglas and Belleville. A new parking lot would be established further along Douglas Street. More trees would come down. An additional acre of garden would be covered by blacktop.

Victorians had already begun to refer to the grounds as "the famous shrunken gardens" when, in August 1962, details of a "multimillion dollar scheme" began to leak out. The CPR was exploring a variety of options: construction of a luxury apartment building, rising to the same height as the Empress, on the lawn along Belleville Street; expansion of the bus terminal into the rose garden; doubling the size of the parking lot and adding a gas station; and building, along Government Street, a "garden shopping arcade." The latter proposal bore an interesting similarity to that made by Herbert Cuthbert in 1900, and just as Cuthbert's idea had failed to win favour more than sixty years earlier, council members rose as one to reject the very idea of replacing the Empress's front lawn with a shopping mall.

The city acted quickly to establish the Inner Harbour Precinct and then passed a series of bylaws governing construction within the area. Setbacks were increased to 100 feet and the height limitation on new buildings was reduced to 70 feet. That put paid to both the shopping arcade and the luxury high rise.

The CPR's real estate manager issued a veiled threat. "If the Empress is to be preserved, it must be allowed the wherewithal to survive. The regulations could, and probably will, defeat their own purpose."

"But," he continued, "I don't want to sound alarming. The situation isn't all *that* alarming."

But, actually, it was.

There was something seriously awry with the hotel's profit picture. In 1961, the Empress produced gross revenues of $2,404,487, but after deductions for operating expenses ($2,161,700), head office charges ($92,000) and depreciation ($183,421), the result was a loss of $32,634. And 1961 was a relatively good year. In 1960, the net loss had been $186,485; in 1963 it would rise to $200,000.

Cyril Chapman was prepared to try almost anything to produce a profit. In July 1960, an electric sign—huge plastic block letters, spelling the words Empress Hotel—was installed over the front entrance on Government Street. "Anyone who doesn't know this is the Empress Hotel shouldn't be staying here!" a long-time guest fumed. But soon he would be encountering a great many guests who did not meet his standards, for the manager had decided to take the Empress Hotel down-market.

Chapman was concerned about the growing popularity of motels and motor lodges and felt that he had no choice but to meet the competition head-on. On 1 August 1961, the hotel was rechristened "Empress Hotel and Motor Lodge," and one hundred rooms in the Humboldt wing were set aside for people who were prepared to handle their own baggage and make do without room service.

With rates in the motor lodge set well below those that applied in the hotel proper ($7.00 for a double room with bath as opposed to $13.50-$21.00), the switchboard was jammed with requests for reservations. By the end of August, Chapman was able to boast that the motor lodge had been "booked solid" since it opened, and the *Colonist* was wondering, "Is the character of the Empress Hotel changing?"

"Women in shorts and slacks are now a familiar sight in the stately lobby," the newspaper fretted. "People wearing dressing gowns over their swimsuits may be seen walking across to the Crystal Garden."

Guests who had been returning to the Empress for years were startled at the changes. "It just doesn't go with the atmosphere of the place," a Vancouver businessman grumbled.

Many staff members agreed. "I must admit it takes a bit of getting used to," one of them sighed. "I can remember the days when most of our guests wore evening dress after 6 P.M."

Leslie Parkinson, who followed Chapman as manager, also followed his lead in pursuing profit-generating schemes, as well as adding a few penny-pinching innovations of his own. He

decided that recorded "piped-in" music would do very well for the Dining Room. Billy Tickle had retired a few years earlier, and his role as leader of the trio had been taken by his pianist, Malcolm More, who had been playing in the Lounge for thirty-five years. When More and the other musicians saw the music outlets being installed in the dining room, they resigned in protest. "One of the guests who had lived here for years took us to dinner when he heard we had resigned," More said. "We went to the Glenshiel Hotel."

Under Parkinson's direction, commercialism, albeit commercialism of a most genteel nature, was introduced to the ground floor when Dorothy Wismer, wife of the former attorney general, opened an antique shop in the former Ladies' Parlour. But the rental charged to Mrs. Wismer would not go very far in reducing the hotel's $200,000 net loss. To do that, Parkinson adopted a bold scheme. He decided to take in other people's washing. In 1964, he outbid the city's three commercial laundries to win the contract for the Veterans' Hospital, an action that raised the ire of existing laundries, earned the hotel masses of bad publicity and produced revenues of only $13,000.

Victorians mourned the passing of a style of life, but at the same time they experienced a feeling of relief. If the CPR was willing to adapt to changing times, then surely the future of the Empress was secure. No one guessed that within three years, the CPR would be thinking the unthinkable.

In 1964, the CPR's board of governors was forced to come to terms with an unpleasant reality. The civic subsidies, under which both the Empress Hotel and the Crystal Garden operated, were nearing their end. And they could not be renewed, neither could a new agreement be negotiated, for the provincial government had passed legislation prohibiting municipalities from providing tax forgiveness or entering into any special arrangements with corporations.

In 1965, the dollar-a-year lease the company was paying for the land under the Crystal Garden would rise to fair market value, and the building would no longer be provided with free water. The Crystal was producing an annual profit of only $7,000 a year. The structure was judged to be "in very poor shape." The bill for repairs and upgrading was expected to reach half a million dollars. The CPR had very little trouble reaching a decision.

"The Crystal Garden is now of little value to the Empress Hotel," the CPR president announced. And with that, he handed the building's keys to the city and walked away from the CPR's $300,000 investment.

The Empress Hotel presented a thornier problem. It was an institution beloved not only by Victorians but also by more than a few members of the CPR's board. But the hotel was losing money, and the taxes, fixed at $34,000 in 1945, would rise to over $80,000 in 1965. And, like the Crystal Garden, the hotel was badly in need of upgrading.

Its furnishings had become tired and worn. As Dick Fagan of the *Oregon Journal* joked, "It had been 25 years since we last stopped at the Empress. We were told that if we happened to get the same room, we'd find the same curtains."

But the most serious problem was much more than simply cosmetic. Since 1908, the hotel had manufactured its own electrical power. On more than a few occasions, when wild winter storms knocked out the city's power, the Empress's independent supply had proved to be a boon to both the hotel's guests and to Victorians. "We never worried when the lights went out," a nearby resident explained. "We always knew we could go to the Empress and get a meal and keep warm." But what had once been an asset had now become a liability.

The electricity produced by the hotel's powerhouse was direct current. Simple to generate and easy to transmit over short distances, direct current had been a reasonable choice when electrical power was required to do little more than illuminate light bulbs. But, by 1965, tourists were travelling with a variety of electrical gadgets—shavers, hair dryers, radios—all of which operated on alternating current and none of which could be connected to the hotel's electrical system without disastrous results. "You plugged your shaver in and, well, it just got fried!"

The Empress coped as best it could. The management located a small supply of direct current radios, which it rented to permanent residents. Light bulbs were changed to lower wattages as the demand for electricity grew, with the result that power was conserved but corridors and hallways became unusually dim. A single line of alternating current, supplied by B.C. Hydro, was run

*Located at the corner of Douglas and Humboldt Streets and connected to the hotel by a 330-foot-long tunnel under Douglas, the power plant provided all the steam and electricity to the Crystal Garden and the Empress Hotel. The laundry, capable of handling a daily load of 22,000 pieces of linen, did the washing for the* Princess *boats as well as for the Empress Hotel.* VICTORIA CITY ARCHIVES PR238

into the hotel to power vacuum cleaners and the Empress's solitary television set. Warning signs, alerting guests to the direct current, were posted by every electrical outlet in every bedroom. A number of "sanitized universal electric razors" were available at the registration desk, but often the supply did not meet the demand. On more than a few occasions, the clerks at the tourist information office found the first question of the day coming from a hotel guest who had stumbled across the street, shaver in hand, asking, "Please, do you have anywhere I can plug this in?"

The Empress was clearly trading on the romance of its past. And worse, its condition was reflecting badly on the company as a whole. Something had to be done. In November 1964, the CPR board of directors gathered in Victoria. "I like this hotel. It is one of the great hostelries in Canada," Chairman N. R. Crump declared. "I hope we can retain the Empress—in one form or another."

Just what form the Empress might take became the subject of a study by a committee composed of members of the CPR's hotel, engineering and real estate departments in collaboration with Leslie Parkinson, the Empress's manager. That study revealed a hotel in desperate straits.

The motor lodge concept had done nothing to improve profits. Room rates had been pared, but operating expenses had remained virtually unchanged. So while occupancy rates had risen, profits had declined. And with some guests expecting either Empress-style charm or motel-style convenience and getting neither, the motor lodge was proving to be a constant source of complaint.

Complaints were also being generated by the hotel's "sprawling and inefficient layout." The location of the Humboldt wing had always been a problem. Because it had been considered unwise to drive new foundation pilings along the north wing after an underground stream was discovered to be running through the site, the Humboldt addition had not been snugged up to the older building. Instead, the hotel had become two separate buildings, with the addition connected to the north wing by a bridge, which appeared to be part of the hotel but was actually only a hallway wide. With the registration desk and lobby located at the porte-cochère entrance, the rooms in the new wing were "miles" from the front desk and from all the hotel's amenities. "The Empress Hotel is like a rabbit warren, a maze of endless corridors," guests grumbled. "You should issue people with a map."

Because the company had failed to allocate adequate capital funds, the condition of the hotel had seriously deteriorated. The furnishings in the public rooms and the bedrooms were "badly worn and obsolete." Many of the bathrooms were "antiquated and unsatisfactory." The corridors were "dingy and unattractive."

To remedy the many problems, the committee members studied a variety of options. One was to do nothing, but that would only lead to loss of patronage and eventual shutdown. The hotel could be modernized and refurbished, but the cost would be high—as much as five million dollars—and even then, the renovation would not correct the basic problems that had been created by the location of the Humboldt wing. The committee considered the possibility of selling but concluded that the Empress had "no value as an operating hotel." If the building were demolished, the vacant land had a theoretical value of between $1,350,000 and $2,400,000, but they doubted that a buyer could be found. The property was simply too large. "Although an assembled parcel of nine acres of prime real estate would command a premium price in most large metropolitan areas, the situation is probably the reverse in Victoria," the CPR concluded.

One suggestion came from the company's general manager of hotels. The Humboldt wing would be retained, but everything else would be demolished and replaced with a new structure housing the lobby, Dining Room, Lounge and convention facilities. The new building could be designed to "blend" with the Humboldt wing and would cost about $3,400,000.

Alternatively—and this was the solution the committee favoured—the Humboldt wing would be saved, but the 1912 south wing and the Conservatory would be torn down. As for the 1908 centre block, the ground floor, containing the public rooms, would be retained, as would the floor above. But everything above that would be demolished. Part of the Lounge would become a cocktail bar, as the Coronet Room would disappear with the demolition of the south wing. An escalator would be installed to carry conventioneers up from the Lounge to the first floor, which would be converted into a "modern convention facility." The Dining Room would remain as a dining room but would assume the duties of the basement coffee shop, which would itself be converted into the registration desk and lobby. All the problems created by the hotel's sprawl would be solved.

Fortunately, before making any final decision, the CPR commissioned independent engineering studies. An analysis of the electrical system revealed that it was costing the Empress $85,000 a year to produce its own power, while the price of purchasing the same amount of power from B.C. Hydro would be only $14,600. In other words, the Empress was paying an extra $70,400 a year to operate its antiquated, irritating, direct-current system.

None of the studies held the Humboldt wing in high esteem. The bathroom fixtures were "old-fashioned," the heating system was "obsolete," ventilation in the bathrooms depended "on the vagaries of the weather," and the water pressure, produced by two gravity storage tanks in the attic, was well below what the engineers considered a basic minimum.

While the Humboldt wing was not quite the asset the committee had considered it to be, the older parts of the building, as reports from a team of structural engineers pointed out, were not nearly so bad as the company had supposed. In fact, some twenty years earlier, the older parts of the building had proven sturdy enough to ride out the worst earthquake in Victoria's recorded history. Measuring 7.3 on the Richter scale and centred off the island's west coast, the quake had struck at 10:14 on Sunday morning, 23 June 1946. In Victoria, sidewalks undulated, plate-glass windows bulged and chimneys collapsed. Room-service waiter Peter Shippen was in a corridor on the fifth floor of the centre block when the ground began to heave. "I was almost thrown off my feet. My shoulder bumped off one wall and then off the other," he remembered. Tiles fell from some bathroom walls, new cracks appeared in ceilings, and a large crack developed between the 1908 section and the 1912 addition, but no serious damage occurred and no serious faults were revealed.

Over the years, the southern part of the building had settled a total of 30 inches, but for the past fifty years, the foundation had been subjected to intensive scrutiny, and the engineers predicted that future settlement would be in the range of only two-and-a-half inches. The existing settlement had produced no serious structural damage and none was expected in the future.

In December 1965, when CPR executives gathered in Victoria to decide the Empress's fate, word leaked out that they were considering demolishing the entire building and replacing it with "a modern, functional high-rise hotel" or a "modern motor-hotel of special design."

"We are well aware of the affection Victorians have for the Empress," a CPR executive informed an apprehensive city council, "but all we have here is a beautiful old building in the middle of a garden. It is costly to operate, it isn't functional, and it is losing the company a lot of money."

"The Grand Old Lady on Government Street has celebrated her 57th birthday. She may not reach retirement," the *Colonist* worried. And the *Hamilton Spectator* warned, "Without this splendid relic of the Edwardian era, literally tens of thousands of tourists will never return. This is the mecca, this is the heart and soul of the city."

The president of Victoria's Chamber of Commerce took his concerns directly to the CPR. "I told them what the Empress meant to us in Victoria, how it was the centre of our lives, how it dominated our lives, how disastrous it would be to lose it. Then we waited breathlessly."

The decision was announced on 10 June 1966. The Empress would not be demolished. Instead, the CPR would embark on a four-million-dollar campaign of renovation and refurbishment. Victoria's mayor was almost overcome with gratitude, wishing the CPR directors "God speed in your important project."

His feelings were shared by Empress supporters across the continent. An editorial in the *Vancouver Province* was typical of the response: "Traditionalists will sigh with relief at the assurances that Victoria's Empress Hotel is not to be dragged all the way into the twentieth century by the current renovation program. World travellers say the Empress echoes the Victorian splendor of hotels in Cairo, Hong Kong and other romantic places; surely this is reason enough to preserve the lavishly wasted space and rampant peculiarities of the 'grand old lady of Government Street.'"

*Chapter Eight*

# OPERATION TEACUP

THE RENOVATION PROGRAM, playfully dubbed Operation Teacup, involved only the older sections of the building. One million dollars would be spent to convert the wiring to alternating current. An additional three million would be spent on updating the public rooms and the bedrooms. As for the Humboldt wing, it would be "amputated" from the rest of the building. No improvements would be made. It would be used only in the summer as "overflow" accommodation.

Operation Teacup was expected to take four years, with most of the work accomplished during the winter months when occupancy was low. Appointed project manager was Alan Tremain, "a breezy, cheery Englishman," who approached the project with an almost unseemly energy and an outspokenness that some former managers might not have found endearing. "When I first saw that coffee shop, I almost lost hope!" he chortled. And he could hardly wait to remove "that Mickey Mouse sign" over the front door.

Tremain moved with lightning speed. By summer of 1967, nine months after work had begun, the coffee shop had become the Garden Cafe; 50 miles of new wiring had been installed; 236 bedrooms had been refurnished, replumbed, redecorated and equipped, for the first time, with television sets.

*The lobby hall, viewed from the Conservatory. During
Operation Teacup, it was converted into a "shopping mall."*
EMPRESS HOTEL ARCHIVES

By December, the new vice-regal suite was ready for unveiling. The suite had been relocated from the Humboldt wing to the second floor of the centre block, where eight rooms had been combined to form the new suite. Hugh Stephen, the mayor of Victoria, had the pleasure of attending the official opening, presided over by the lieutenant-governor, General George Pearkes. "We looked it over, and we were all very impressed. Then Mrs Pearkes said, 'I'd love to see the honeymoon suite.' And the manager bowed, 'Certainly, Mrs. Pearkes,' and we all traipsed upstairs. It was pretty obvious that the room was occupied, but we all looked around, and as I was coming out I saw this young couple sort of hovering in the corridor. I went up to them and said, 'I'm the mayor of Victoria. How nice that you've come to stay in our city.' And then I turned around and said, 'Oh, and this is His Honour the Lieutenant-Governor, General Pearkes, and Mrs. Pearkes. And this is Hugh Curtis, the mayor of Saanich.' "

It is unlikely that any other honeymooners were treated to such a welcome, but if their tastes ran to red plush, flocked wallpaper and plastic trelliswork, they must have been well-pleased with the new bridal suite.

Victorians, who had been sorry to see most of the greenhouses come down to make way for more parking, were beginning to wonder if their support of Operation Teacup had been misplaced when attention shifted to the ground floor and work began on what Tremain enthusiastically described as a "shopping mall." The front desk, which had run half the length of the wide hallway leading to the Conservatory, was compressed into a small area by the porte-cochère entrance and, in its place, a row of shops was installed.

The Palm Court would be boxed in on two sides by shops, with the backs of those shops intruding so far into the room that the domed ceiling appeared seriously off-centre. Tremain promised that the stained-glass dome would remain. But then, in the winter of 1968, the city was struck by an unusually heavy snowfall, and the glass, unable to support the burden of snow and ice, came crashing down into the Palm Court and shattered into thousands of pieces. The framework remained in place, but there was no money in the budget for restoration. And so the dome was hidden—"entombed," some people said—above a lowered "strikingly inelegant" ceiling.

Just as the Palm Court lost all its natural light, so too did the Crystal Ballroom. The glass doors that had separated it from the Palm Court were replaced by heavy oak-panelled doors 12 feet high. The skylight roof was replaced by one clad in copper, through which no light penetrated. In the barrel-vaulted ceiling, glass panels that had been cracked or broken were replaced with plywood. Then the plywood panels and the remaining glass panels were covered with a heavy coat of powder blue paint.

The dignified Dining Room became a dinner-dance cabaret, due, in part, to CPR chairman N. R. Crump's affection for the room. Originally, it had been planned to hide air-conditioning ducts above a lowered ceiling. But when Operation Teacup was about to get underway, Crump had informed the manager, "I don't care what you do, but don't touch that ceiling!" And so a section of the floor was raised to carry the ductwork. With the addition of a carved oak balustrade, the raised floor became a dining platform. The centre of the room became a dance floor, and along one wall a small stage was built. The portraits of the wives of the Governors General, which had been a feature of the Dining Room for forty years, projected too prim an image for a room devoted to cabaret, and so down they came, to be rehung in a lower level hallway.

Aware of local concerns, some of which were expressed by "howls of protest," Leslie Parkinson began to place reassuring progress reports in Victoria's newspapers. In Vancouver and other cities, he launched a promotional campaign featuring the slogan "The Old Girl Goes MOD!"

When they learned how their hotel was being described, many Victorians felt insulted. Ainslie Helmcken, a great-grandson of James Douglas, was incensed. "Those who like myself regard the Grand Old Lady as just as much a Victoria institution as the Parliament Buildings can only recoil in horror at such patent nonsense," he thundered. "Whoever is responsible for the promotional advertising for the Empress Hotel should be taken out on to the Causeway and there be publicly shot!"

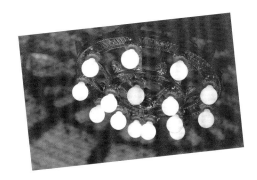

"I authorized the placing of the advertisement," Leslie Parkinson admitted. "Of course, it was meant to be taken lightheartedly rather than literally. The Empress is now more comfortable, more contemporary; not one whit less dignified." That was only partly true. The hotel's promotion department had become carried away by the ethos of the early 1960s—Carnaby Street, swinging London, Mary Quant and miniskirts. But the attempt to project a youthful image suggested instead that the Empress did not know how to grow old gracefully. Travel writers were quick to make an unflattering comparison. The once stately Empress began to be described with phrases such as "the old lady is swinging" and "the dowager lifts her skirts." Victoria's "grand old lady of Government Street" was in danger of becoming an object of fun.

Now that he had a hotel of which he could be proud, manager Leslie Parkinson went in pursuit of the convention business.

Not that the hotel had not been attractive to conventioneers in the past. In 1941, the Empress had welcomed over a thousand delegates to a gathering of the Philanthropic Educational Organization Sisterhood. "It was amazing," a maid remembered. "Every room full. And not so much as one glass broken." Not all conventioneers were quite so well behaved. A few years later, when the Shriners came to the Empress, they took over the Lounge, drowning out the mellow sounds of Billy Tickle with their raucous clown band.

Victoria realtor Eric Charman remembered another convention that might have been more trouble than it was worth. "I went to see Cyril Chapman and said, 'You know I think that I can get the Junior Chamber of Commerce convention for you!' Well, Chapman was thrilled. He didn't know that no one wanted the Chamber. I mean, back then, they were all a bunch of drunks."

The manager began to get the picture when the Calgary delegation arrived—aboard a horse-drawn chuck wagon. When the horses were released to graze on the Empress's manicured front lawn, Cyril Chapman's blood pressure began to rise. He was driven to something close to apoplexy over the antics of the "wake-up" committee.

"We went to Safeway and borrowed some of their shopping carts," Eric Charman remembered. "We filled them with bottles of aspirins, hangover remedies, Bloody Marys and stuff like that, all ready to be delivered in the morning. Chapman gave us a list of about forty room numbers and said, 'Now, you mustn't go anywhere *near* these rooms. They belong to the permanent residents, and they *mustn't* be disturbed.' Well, we considered that to be very helpful advice. And of course those were the *only* rooms we went to. Chapman had his hands full that day."

Many conventioneers were sober and industrious, and even those who were inclined to be rowdy filled off-season bedrooms that would otherwise have been empty. In 1966, the Empress had welcomed 11,000 delegates to 66 conventions. Now, with the hotel rewired and its major public rooms redone, the management redoubled its efforts to lure conventioneers.

"Now gone mod!" the hotel's convention literature proclaimed. "The Empress has taken on the Twentieth Century without losing a smidgen of her charm and dignity."

But the character of all the major rooms—the Lounge, the Palm Court, the Crystal Ballroom, the Dining Room—had been diminished by Operation Teacup. In fact, Leslie Parkinson had almost succeeded in ridding the hotel of one of the more important elements of its charm, its delightfully eccentric permanent residents.

During the first phase of Operation Teacup, all the residents were required to vacate their rooms. They were not amused. "We are none of us moving," they told the *Victoria Times* in November 1966.

"But they did," Parkinson reported triumphantly a few weeks later, explaining that he had pointed out to the "dear old ladies" that he had control of their water, their light and their heat.

Some of them moved out of the hotel entirely, but others simply shifted to other rooms while the work progressed. Like the McMillans, who had been residents for over twenty years, they could not imagine living anywhere else.

Among the residents who managed to cope with the ravages of Operation Teacup were Edward Stimson and his wife. Taken together or apart, the Stimsons presented a singular appearance. Tall and gaunt and always wearing a long coat that flapped around his ankles, Edward Stimson resembled nothing so much as a scarecrow. Mrs. Stimson's habitual attire was a seersucker cloak gathered on a ribbon, topped with a hat shaped like an inverted coal scuttle. Winter or summer, their wardrobe never changed. The Stimsons were always cold. The hotel's steam heat raised to "roasting" the temperature of their small single room, but it was never hot enough. Not hot enough for the Stimsons and, they were convinced, not hot enough to ripen the green bananas they bought in bulk.

To staff members driven backwards from their door by the heavy smell of overripe bananas, Mrs. Stimson explained, "You see, this way we don't *need* to eat in the Dining Room."

People like the Stimsons did not fit with the hotel's new "swinging" image. They were not asked to leave, but neither were they encouraged to stay. Some residents left for their permanent reward, others were driven out by rising prices. Soon there was only one permanent resident left, and she was the most extraordinary of them all.

It was in the late 1960s and Cybil Martin was a widow in her seventies when realtor Eric Charman suggested she sell her house and move to the Empress. He negotiated a unique arrangement. Cybil would pay all the expenses involved in adapting the rooms to meet her requirements in exchange for a long lease.

Cybil took over the entire top floor of the south wing. Walls were demolished and money was poured in to create several thousand square feet of gracious living space in which she lived the life of a grande dame, enjoying a standard of luxury unique in the hotel's history.

On one occasion, soon after she had sold her car and fired her chauffeur, she invited friends to a private luncheon at the Union Club. Although the club was less than a block away, she had no intention of arriving on foot. But by the time a taxi arrived to collect her, her guests were already gathered at the club waiting to be greeted. Cybil considered that a breach of etiquette, and she was determined that it would never happen again.

Later that afternoon, she informed the Empress's manager of the action she had taken. "I've decided to hire another chauffeur," she said. "That new young doorman you think so highly of? I've decided to hire him."

"Oh, Mrs. Martin," the manager groveled. "I don't think he'll take it."

"Well, actually," Cybil purred, "he already has. I've sent him to buy a car. I was going to buy a Cadillac, but he preferred a Mercedes-Benz. He's gone off to buy one now. And you know, he didn't seem to mind at all when I told him that he would have to spend half the year with me in Florida."

In the 1980s, when her lease expired, she chose not to renew it. "I am tired of stumbling over suitcases every afternoon when I come down for cocktails," she said. And the Empress lost its last permanent resident and a reliable income of $24,000 a year.

It was left to Louis Finamore, who became manager in 1968, to complete Operation Teacup by coming to grips with the problem of the Humboldt wing. During the first phase of Operation Teacup, the 1929 wing had been ignored. There had been no renovations, no upgrading. During the winter, it was shut off from the rest of the hotel. Its use in the summer resulted in many complaints. Guests were unhappy with the direct current and with the "shabby furnishings" and the "depressing rooms."

The manager was reluctant to send guests to the Humboldt wing, but if he did not, then the Empress was limited to only 250 rooms. There was talk around town that another hotel chain was preparing to fill the void. "There is obviously greater likelihood of them being frightened off if they are faced with a 430 room Empress Hotel, rather than a 250 room hotel," the CPR's research department pointed out.

In January 1970, plans for the Humboldt wing were announced. The wiring and plumbing would be upgraded. The rooms would be refurbished. And, in recognition of changing times, a new use would be found for the sample rooms on the ground floor.

In earlier years, salesmen had travelled from city to city, setting up shop in sample rooms and inviting retailers to inspect their wares. But now, wholesalers were finding it more efficient to set up displays at trade fairs in larger cities and have merchants from smaller centres come to them. And so it made sense to convert the Empress's sample rooms into a different kind of commercial space. Some were adapted to retail use, including the "Prince Albert" Collection of Miniatures which opened on Humboldt Street. At the northwest corner of the building, the hotel ended its "draught drought" by opening its first beer parlour, a rustically furnished room known as the Beaver.

Finamore also tackled the Coronet Room. Initially, Operation Teacup had envisioned it as "a hearty English pub" to which only men would be admitted. To provide for women and couples, the former Ladies' Parlour had been converted into a cocktail lounge. The details of the ornate plaster ceiling, admired by Rudyard Kipling sixty years earlier, were picked out in red, gold and blue paint, and, after the original plan to name it "Talk of the Town" was dropped, the room settled into a comfortable existence as the Library Bar, an identity it continued to enjoy even after the idea of a "men only" pub was abandoned.

For the Coronet Room, Finamore decided to acknowledge the hotel's having been named after Queen Victoria, Empress of India, by adopting an Indian theme. The Coronet Room became the Bengal Bar; waiters were garbed in Nehru jackets and caps; the menu included a variety of curries, and the cocktail list featured the Bombay Stinger, the Bengal Tiger, the Tropical Itch and the Bengal Bar Special, a lethal mixture of rye, curaçao, pernod and Dubonnet.

The Bengal Bar was an instant success. It became the place to be. The best place to lobby politicians, and the best place to catch sight of John Wayne, who made it a habit to visit the bar

The Library Bar (in the former Ladies' Parlour) was the
most welcome of the many changes produced by Operation Teacup.
Intimate and inviting, it encouraged quiet conversation.

every time he sailed his converted minesweeper, the *Wild Goose*,
into the harbour. One Victoria realtor found that he was con-
ducting so much business out of the bar that he had a personal
phone line installed.

With the success of the Bengal Bar under his belt,
Finamore turned his attention to the youth market. "We had
to do something to liven the place up," he said. "It was too
stodgy." He decided to convert a storage area, formerly used by
the hotel's painters, into a nightclub. "I had nothing in the budget for that kind of thing," he remembered. "We had to do the
best we could with what we had." The room was painted black,
black sofas were ranged along the walls, and coloured lights
were installed in sections of black-painted stovepipe. The
room was christened the Paint Cellar, and rock music began to
reverberate through the Empress's lower halls.

"The Grande Dame of Victoria is wearing Hot Pants," the
*Seattle Post-Intelligencer* quipped.

By 1971, Operation Teacup was officially complete, but some
guests felt that it should have gone further. That June, the
Empress bedded the most significant gathering of Canadian
politicians in its history when the provincial premiers gathered
in Victoria to meet with Prime Minister Pierre Trudeau for a
Constitutional Conference. Trudeau and his wife, Margaret,
were installed in the vice-regal suite, and the premiers were dis-
persed throughout the building—all except William Davis, the
premier of Ontario, who did not think much of the new,
improved Empress. "When he discovered that his room wasn't
air-conditioned, he walked out," the assistant manager recalled.

But then, for all the publicity it generated, Operation
Teacup had never been intended as a complete, thorough renovation. Except for the wiring, some updated plumbing and the
air-conditioning of some of the public rooms, much of the
work was cosmetic—new curtains, new carpets, new paint.

Don Corner discovered as much when he visited the hotel
in 1982. He had been at the Empress some years earlier, and that
was a visit he was not likely to forget. He was sitting in the coffee shop at 8:30 in the evening of 11 October 1955, when a man
wearing a handkerchief mask walked up to the cashier, Evelyn
Coles, brandished a pistol and announced, "This is a holdup."

"I didn't do anything," Evelyn said. "I thought he was fooling."

"I mean business," he shouted. And he fired a shot into the ceiling.

Fifty patrons sat stunned as Evelyn scooped $285 into a paper bag and then watched in silence as the robber ran out the door.

Twenty-seven years later, Don Corner was back in the coffee shop telling friends about the holdup. "One of them scoffed at my story," he recalled. "The waitress at our table took him by the hand and walked him over to show him the bullet hole in the ceiling."

Victoria's fire department also recognized that Operation Teacup had not been a thorough upgrading. In September 1978, the fire inspector marched into the Empress and posted bright orange notices in the lobby, informing guests of deficiencies affecting the safety of the building. The fire-alarm system was obsolete. There were no heat detectors in the hallways. There were too few fire doors.

Ted Balderson, who had assumed the duties of manager a few years earlier, was not pleased. "I don't particularly like the idea of slapping up notices like that," he grumbled. But he was prepared to do whatever was necessary to bring the Empress up to standard, even though a preliminary estimate suggested that the costs might be as high as $650,000. Within three years, Balderson would discover that it had been money well spent.

On 31 January 1981, the hotel was busy, with almost five hundred registered guests, many of whom were attending a veterans' convention. At 3:30 in the morning, an arsonist crept up to the first floor and set fire to the curtains on a hallway window. The recently installed heat and smoke detectors awakened the guests and alerted the desk. The new fire-separation doors prevented the blaze from spreading.

Most of the guests made their own way to fire escapes or were led to safety by firemen. A few had the added excitement of being picked off their window sills by the fire department's aerial ladder. They were forced to spend ninety minutes shivering on the lawn in the chill morning air before being allowed to return to their rooms, but there were no injuries.

The fire had been dangerously intense. The chandeliers in the hallway had fallen from the ceiling and melted into "big globs of brass." The new fire-protection devices had obviously played a role, but even the fire department credited the hotel's age—its solid seventy-three-year-old doors and its lack of air-conditioning, which might have carried smoke throughout the building—with helping to avert a tragedy.

TOP *Library Bar menu cover.* EMPRESS HOTEL ARCHIVES

BOTTOM *In 1971, rock music was introduced to the Empress with the opening of the Paint Cellar nightclub.* EMPRESS HOTEL ARCHIVES

Chapter Nine

# A ROYAL RESTORATION

IN JANUARY 1983, THE EMPRESS HOTEL CELEBRATED its seventy-fifth birthday with an enthusiasm that had been notably lacking when it passed other milestones. A gala anniversary ball was held in the Crystal Ballroom. Victoria's city council declared "Empress Week" and convened in the Lounge for a special meeting.

To mark the occasion, the *Colonist* described the hotel's role in a reverent editorial: "Stately, imposing, marvellously dotty, the Empress is to Victoria what Big Ben is to London, or the Eiffel Tower to Paris—a landmark and a symbol." But the editor, like most Victorians, was familiar only with the public rooms. Behind the scenes, the Empress was rather less than "stately" and "imposing."

According to the executive housekeeper, Paul Jeffery, "The place was a shambles. The roof was leaking. The carpets were worn right through to the floorboards. The draperies were hanging in shreds, water-damaged and sun-damaged. The windows wouldn't open or close. The sills were all chipped. The doors didn't fit properly."

It was just as well, then, that when Hollywood came calling, the Empress was not required to look elegant. (That would come later, in 1992, when the film *Knight Moves*, a grim little thriller featuring Christopher Lambert and Diane Lane, included several scenes filmed in the restored Palm Court and Lounge.)

In 1984, Mickey Rourke arrived at the Empress to film *Year of the Dragon*, in which he played a New York police captain who was "waging a private battle against the chaos on his turf."

Victoria's Chinatown masqueraded as "the secret heart of New York's Chinatown," and the Empress's sub-basement was disguised as a bean-sprout factory. Sheets of plastic were draped between the huge concrete piers that support the building, and the floor was covered with vast vats of water containing sprouting soybeans and several "corpses." Some time after the movie people had packed up and gone home, the desk began to receive complaints about an unpleasant odour. "The bean sprouts!" a staff member exclaimed. "They'd just walked away and left them. We had about a ton of rotting bean sprouts down there. The smell was unbelievable."

Transitory problems were understandable, but Jeffery described an ongoing situation Victorians would have found difficult to believe. "We were sending our laundry to a commercial laundry, but we didn't have enough money to pay them to work on weekends. And we didn't have enough circulating inventory to last for two days." Every Saturday morning, Jeffery and the assistant housekeeper collected all the soiled towels and facecloths and loaded them into the hotel van. "We took them to the James Bay Laundromat. We'd stuff all eleven washing machines, and we'd do the hotel's washing. But even then there were times we'd have to leave rooms vacant because we simply did not have enough linen."

The deteriorating condition of the Empress was the result of a corporate policy that regarded the company's hotels as chronic money losers, coupled with shareholder reluctance to send good money after bad. But then, in the mid-1980s, a series of events occurred, almost simultaneously, and the situation began to change.

The first was the transfer of the hotel company to Canadian Pacific Airlines. Dick Huisman, marketing manager for the airlines, became executive vice-president of CP Hotels. His initial impression of the Empress was not good. He visited the hotel, convened a meeting and sat down on a chair that sported a thick wad of chewing gum. His mood was already grim when he was taken on a tour of the hotel.

It fell to Paul Jeffery to lead Huisman through the Empress. "He opened the doors and saw pink walls and blue ceilings, and he just about went insane. 'Who approved these colour-boards?' he demanded. He'd pull a bedspread off and see the ratty sheets and yell, 'What the hell is this?' By the time he'd finished with the first floor, he'd almost lost his mind."

CP Airlines had already concluded that the hotels needed a major infusion of capital when the airline itself was sold. CP Hotels, which had not been included in the deal, once again became the responsibility of the parent company. It so happened that the new CP president, Bill Stinson, was prepared to solve the problem of the hotels, once and for all. They would be sold or they would be improved. There were no other choices. Fortunately, at the time this decision was being made, tourism was booming and other hotel chains were reaping high profits. In addition, many of the company's hotels had survived unfashionable middle age to become appreciated as "historic" and "distinctive." In the end, the company made a truly momentous decision. It would spend $600 million to restore and renovate its hotels.

At about the same time CP Hotels committed itself to restoring the Empress, the city of Victoria, finally and at last, decided to do something about the city's lack of convention facilities.

Twenty years earlier, the city had realized that it was at a disadvantage in the competition to attract major conferences and conventions. There was no meeting place capable of providing a space for even mid-sized conventions of from 600 to 1,200 people. (In 1941, the PEO convention had been accommodated only after the pool in the Crystal Garden was drained to provide seating for the thousand delegates.) But recognizing a need and actually doing something about filling it were two very different things. Over the years, proposals surfaced, bobbed about for a while and then sank.

But by the mid-1980s, the time was right. Canadian Pacific was not only prepared to invest millions in the Empress but also was anxious to protect that investment, and the city had galvanized itself to look at any valid option. An agreement was reached whereby a conference centre, funded by the provincial and federal governments, would be built on the Empress grounds on land leased by the city for a dollar a year. The new centre would be physically linked to the Empress through the Conservatory, and the hotel would be granted the food and beverage contract. Now, any major renovation and rethinking of the hotel could be done in conjunction with the new conference centre.

In August 1986, an architectural team composed of Calgary-based Steve Carruthers, who was working on the Banff Springs Hotel and the Chateau Lake Louise, and a Vancouver architectural firm, Billington, Poon, whose work included the Saskatoon City Hospital and the Victoria General Hospital, began to prepare a master plan.

On 2 December 1987, the details were revealed. The Empress was to be restored "to its original splendour" at a cost of $32 million. Renovations would include a "new Palm Court, new Crystal Ballroom, 50 new bedrooms, new swimming pool, and new landscaping"—and last, but far from least, a "new entrance and lobbies."

One of the more significant components of the project involved the attempt to solve the problems created by the location of the Humboldt wing. Where the bridge had connected the 1929 wing to the centre block, a new tower, housing elevators and additional bedrooms, would be constructed. Below the tower, a guest-registration lobby, described rather grandly as an "entry pavilion," would be built.

The additions would achieve two goals. Registered guests would enter the hotel at a location that was more central than the traditional porte-cochère entrance, and they would be separated from the Lounge and the guests who were enjoying afternoon tea.

To connect the new registration lobby to the public rooms, all of which were in the centre block, a ramp would be built from the mezzanine level of the new lobby to the hotel's ground floor. Unfortunately, the best position for the ramp would result in the Dining Room being carved in two. The part of the room that faced west over the harbour would become a bar, the Lobby Lounge, while the remainder of the room would continue to function as a dining room.

*The logo created for the hotel's 75th Anniversary in 1983.*
EMPRESS HOTEL ARCHIVES

Work started on the Humboldt wing in the spring of 1988. Rooms without views were developed as "standard" rooms for business travellers. Rooms facing the harbour, including the former vice-regal suite, became twenty-six "heritage" suites, furnished with antique and custom-made reproduction furniture and featuring lavish use of floral-printed chintz in shades of dusty rose and apple green.

By August 1988, the Humboldt wing was ready for unveiling. "Rich furniture finishes, chintz-draped windows, brass fittings and ornamental lighting all give even the smallest room the concentrated lushness of a Fabergé egg," a visitor declared.

Attention now shifted to the older part of the hotel. Such was the magnitude of the project that it was impossible for the hotel to remain open. A new kitchen, costing $3 million, was to be installed. On the lower level, all the private meeting rooms were to be converted to new uses. And on the ground floor, truly major work was planned, particularly in the Palm Court and the Crystal Ballroom.

On 23 October 1988, the Empress closed its doors for the first time in its eighty-year history, and the "Royal Renovation," a race against the clock to meet the reopening target date of April 1989, got underway.

*From the time the project was announced in December 1987 until work began in October 1988, the design of the new tower and particularly of the entrance lobby underwent several changes. The roofline of the lobby was softened, the overall design was simplified, and the driveway was realigned.*

EMPRESS HOTEL ARCHIVES

The philosophy behind the Royal Renovation was as far from the 1960s Operation Teacup as can be imagined. This time, the emphasis was on quality workmanship rather than making do. No attempt was made to give the hotel a new image. Instead, the goal was to restore the Empress to its original elegance. Archival research and on-site examination revealed hidden secrets. In the Palm Court, some of the decorative plasterwork was discovered to have survived the installation of the lowered ceiling, and moulds were taken so that the entire ceiling could be restored. While no written records were found, a comparison of old photographs suggested that the dome featuring coronets in amber glass, which had come crashing down into the Palm Court in 1968, was not the original; and so the decision was made to replicate, as closely as possible, its more intricately patterned predecessor. A room on the lower level that had been walled off and almost forgotten was reopened and adapted to display Empress memorabilia. In other rooms, walled-in fireplaces were uncovered and decorative mouldings were discovered above lowered ceilings. Here and there throughout the hotel, almost a hundred light fixtures dating from 1908 were discovered, reconditioned and rehung. Sixteen of the Lounge's original ram's-head lights were refurbished and rewired, and thirty-four solid brass replicas produced. Given the time frame and the expense involved, the commitment to historical accuracy was really quite extraordinary.

As work progressed, costs rose. More pilings than originally specified had to be driven to support the new tower. And it was discovered that the ivy covering the building had done more damage than had been supposed.

Although the Empress had always been described as "ivy-covered," the vines planted in 1908 were a variety of Virginia creeper, which had, as a building cover, the advantage of being deciduous. In the mid-1950s, the creeper had been killed off by a severe frost and was replaced with a true ivy, an evergreen ivy that held the Empress in a damp embrace throughout the year, never allowing the brickwork to dry. The ivy had worked its way between the bricks, carrying moisture into the walls.

By December, manager Ian Barbour, who had been brought in to oversee the project, was suggesting that to correct those and other problems, an extra ten million dollars would have to be spent.

A few weeks later, with three months to go before the scheduled opening day, an observer reported: "Stepping into the Empress Hotel lobby is like walking through a bombed-out war zone. Gusts of wind howl through open doors and windows, sheets of plastic dangle from the ceiling, hunks of old plaster litter the floor, and there is an acrid smell of paint, glue and solvent."

But Barbour was confident that the project would be finished on time and that the final result would be impressive. "I think people will be overwhelmed when they see the hotel," he predicted. And that proved to be true.

The Crystal Ballroom was glorious. The skylight roof had not been reinstalled, but the restoration had accomplished the next best thing. The barrel-vaulted ceiling had been dismantled, the glass had been removed, and the putty scoured out of every frame. Then the frames had been repaired, glaziers had installed mirrors, and the entire ceiling had been put back in place. "It took 141 days to finish that job," the site co-ordinator remembered. The crystal chandeliers had been restored to their former brilliance. Each chandelier had been dismantled, cleaned and restrung, an enormous job that had taken four people two months to accomplish.

The Palm Court was a revelation. The shops that had backed into the space had disappeared, and the room had regained its original proportions. Separated only by wide glass doors, it had become part of the Lounge once again. And best of all, the ugly lowered ceiling was gone and the glass dome had been recreated, featuring motifs in tan and beige with highlights of green, blue, pink, red and mauve. It had taken ten craftsmen five months to complete, and the results were spectacular.

Overall, the impression was of light and colour. Of the Palm Court suffused with the gentle glow of the stained-glass dome; of walls bathed in shades of shell pink and warm rose; of lavender, gold and startling blue combined together to pick out previously unnoticed features.

The job of dressing the Empress was given to Dallas-based interior designer Deborah Lloyd Forrest. "When you think about something marvellous from the past, you tend to embellish it," she explained. "The memory often becomes more rosy than it ever really was. I see the unfolding of this project in the same way—as a recreation of an embellished memory."

Never in its history had the Empress appeared quite so glamorous. Never before had the Lounge boasted quite so many potted palms. And never before had quite so much fabric been used to decorate its windows. But the whole look of the place seemed, somehow, right.

*Chapter Ten*

# INTO THE

# TWENTY-FIRST CENTURY

WHEN THE EMPRESS REOPENED after the Royal Renovation, it seemed as though everyone—including a very unexpected visitor—wanted to see the results. At midnight on a March night in 1992, a taxi driver reported to the parking attendant that he had seen a cougar slip into the parkade. Just a Great Dane, scoffed the attendant, but the driver was adamant: he knew a cougar when he saw one. Convinced, the attendant closed the gate and called for help.

Police constable and wildlife photographer Gary Green joined the conservation officer who was summoned to deal with the beast. "We had tranquilizer guns and weapons to destroy the cougar if we had to. We went in with the dogs [bluetick coonhounds Jessie and Striker] and handler and the cougar came out. We fired one dart and the cat was still hissing, so we fired another one, and it went under a heating vent and collapsed. We were just going to put the handcuffs on it when it twitched—you've never seen three grown men back up so fast. We fired another dart, and then we carried it out."

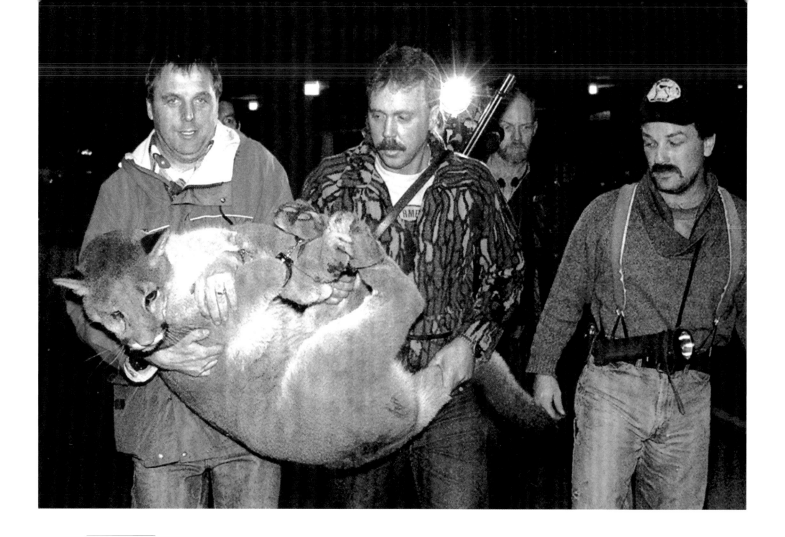

Outside the parking garage, a crowd of about fifty people awaited. "There was a great cheer as we came out," recalls Green. "Everyone was so happy it could be captured alive. We let one woman stroke it, and she said that was the most fabulous experience of her life, to touch a wild cougar." The adolescent male cat was released back into the wild at the west end of Cowichan Lake, and the story of the hotel's midnight prowler ran in newspapers around the globe. The errant cougar is recreated in a hotel crest emblazoned on the stained glass window above the door to the Library.

As far as staff know, a bear has never made it to the Empress, but a man in bear costume did: in 1995, as guide outfitters met in the adjoining Conference Centre, a member of the conservation group Bear Watch dressed in a furry costume hung out a fifth-floor window while he and a second man unfurled a banner protesting bear hunting.

Ten years later, a droopy-eared basset hound put the Empress back into the news from Vancouver to Nova Scotia when she wandered into the lobby, alone and wearing no identification. "If you want a free night at the Empress Hotel, you'd better have big brown eyes, long velvety ears and four legs," reported the *Times Colonist* the next day. "She didn't have a credit card or a reservation, but night manager Jose Guidoriagao checked in Lucy anyway." Hotel staff provided the two-year-old with a dog bed, blankets, a silver water bowl and dog treats, and she stayed at the hotel until her owner spotted her on a newscast the following night.

Dogs might have come in handy in the winter of 1996, when hotel employees used everything but sled dogs to get to work after Victoria's massive snowfall. Andrew Leslie, the hotel's chief engineer, was duty manager the night of 29 December. When he went to sleep, light snow was falling; when he awoke, more than a metre—drifting to almost two metres—clogged Victoria's streets, overwhelming the city for three days. Nothing moved: not ploughs in a city more used to cherry blossoms than snow drifts, not delivery trucks and certainly not guests, who were snowbound for the duration.

"They were only ploughing routes for fire and ambulance. You couldn't get in or out," Leslie recalls. "The guests that were here couldn't get to the ferry." Employees on shift when the snow fell stayed; some of those off-shift made it to the hotel on snowshoes or skis, and some slogged their way through the deep, heavy snow on foot. "They were dead tired by the time they got here. Some employees went to help at the old folks' home just up the hill; they just had their night shift in, two or three people."

Food was a problem, but hotel employees set up a buffet line for three meals a day. By the third day, when supplies were running out, the executive chef walked through the snow to a supermarket ten blocks away for bread and milk. "For the guests, it was just an event. They were very appreciative of our efforts. We didn't go changing sheets, because there was no one to do it, but they could do it themselves if they wanted to." And some management employees quickly learned how to polish mirrors and clean bathrooms. Guests and employees celebrated New Year's at the hotel; by the following day, enough streets had been cleared for life to return to close to normal.

The lighter side of Empress life made the headlines through the 1990s, but so did more serious stories. In September, 1999, the Empress closed its doors for only the second time ever—the first was for the Royal Renovation—as employees went on strike, seeking wage parity with employees at the Hotel Vancouver and other contract concessions. The story was front-page news across the country, but the strike was settled in little more than a week, and employees returned to work. On the picket line, they had kept in practice, serving tea to passersby.

Afternoon tea at the Empress was, after all, synonymous with Victoria for people around the world. In 1996, *Good Morning America*, the top-rated U.S. morning television show, came to Victoria to do one of five programs on Canada and broadcast from the tea lobby. For the first time in the history of the hotel, afternoon tea took place in the early morning, as Canadian musician and songwriter Sarah McLachlan sang and the Canadian Scottish Regiment Pipes and Drums tuned up outside.

A myriad of travel journalists wrote about tea at the hotel as one of the city's two essential experiences (the other was visiting The Butchart Gardens.) Some hundred thousand people confirmed that assertion every year, sipping tea and eating cakes and sandwiches. For a brief time, the hotel even experimented with serving tea in the evening, for the benefit of cruise-ship passengers whose crowded itineraries did not allow for tea between the traditional hours of 2 and 5 P.M. On occasion, when demand exceeded supply in the tea lobby, or

*Heavy snow blocked access to the hotel in the winter of 1996.*

TONY OWEN

when a large group made a reservation, tea was also served in the Library, in the Palm Court, on the verandah or in one of the restaurants.

"Afternoon tea is an experience, not just a meal," notes hotel general manager Roger Soane, a fact immediately obvious to comic-book characters Betty and Veronica, who came to tea at the Empress in a 1996 *Archie* comic book set in Canada. Two years later, John Travolta also took tea, but reporters were turned away when they sought an audience. "He's here, and he's having tea," an employee austerely confirmed, but he did not want to be approached by anyone, staff included.

The dress code for afternoon tea has softened considerably since the early days, when men wore suits and ladies wore dresses, and even since the days when jeans were forbidden attire. "People were wearing jeans that probably cost $100," recalls Deirdre Campbell, public relations manager from 1991 to 1998, "and we said, 'Sorry, you'll have to change into these $25 polyester pants.' Some people had fun with it, but some were put out." The dress code changed to "smart casual:" no short shorts or flip-flops, but no requirement for white gloves or ties.

Marlene Watson has worked at the Empress for almost forty years, becoming a full-time tea server some thirty years ago. "When I first started, it was English muffins or crumpets, sandwiches or fruit salad, layer cake and tea. Now we have scones, sandwiches, pastries." Gone also are the days when the server anointed a "tea mother" to serve at each table—now the server pours the tea.

But afternoon tea traditions are still strong. Since 1998, tea has been served on the Empress china. The first set of the ornate Royal Doulton china is reputed to have been presented to King George V in 1914 when he officially opened the Booth factory that produced it. The pattern was initially used at the Empress in 1939, at the head table when King George VI and Queen Elizabeth dined in the Empress Room with 250 guests, and used again when Princess Elizabeth visited the Empress the year before her coronation as Queen in 1952. Royal Doulton now makes the china, with gold detail hand painted, exclusively for the Empress.

Equally important is the Empress brand tea. Although there are now eight blends of tea available, ranging from Earl Grey to orange pineapple, most people still choose the signature blend—Assam, Kenyan black and Kenyan green, South Indian, Sri Lankan Dimbula, and Keemum—a tea described as having "burgundy depth," "light oaky notes" and "hint of floral flavour" and which "takes milk exceedingly well" (milk poured into the cup first, of course).

For Marlene Watson, the experience of serving tea is a source of endless satisfaction, as those who take tea at her tables become friends. "I've got addresses—not that I'll ever get there—from Hawaii, Vienna, Texas; they write to me, send me a calendar with pictures of what they have done all year."

And the Empress itself is special to her. "It's like my second home. A lot of the staff have worked together for a long time; I probably see more of them than I see of my own family. The longer you work here, the more you feel like the hotel is a little bit yours."

*Marlene Watson serves the hotel's
famed afternoon tea in the tea lobby.*
THE FAIRMONT EMPRESS/
TONY OWEN

Although tradition continued to be a big part of the hotel's existence, so did change, as the Empress moved with trends in the hospitality industry. In 1998, the hotel celebrated its ninetieth birthday. By then, it was clear that the existing ownership structure was not serving the Empress and the other Canadian Pacific hotels well. That year, CP was split into five different companies, including a rail company and a hotel company. Management recognized that, in an increasingly international business, the hotels needed an international presence. CP Hotels bought Princess Hotels, with properties in Mexico, Arizona, Bermuda and Barbados, and in 1999 bought Fairmont Hotels, a small chain of heritage properties in major U.S. cities. The group was renamed Fairmont Hotels and Resorts, and the Empress became the Fairmont Empress.

Empress general manager Roger Soane explains the move as a response to the need for an internationally recognized name. "People used to seek out individuals, the great butcher, the little boutique hotel. But now, everything in business has gone away from the independents. We are all so brand conscious. The majority of people live their lives in brands, from cars to shoes to shirts to coffee."

Guests appreciated the individuality they found in Fairmont's hotels—all different, all classic, with no cookie-cutter rooms or faceless service—but they also wanted the reassurance and the familiarity that came from a brand name. As well, being part of a larger chain brought economies in staffing, promotion and purchasing.

A trend in the arcane financial world saw hotels owned by one company, managed by another. Throughout various changes in ownership, though, the companies that owned and managed the Empress continued to keep their headquarters in Canada, thus preserving the hotel's Canadian tradition.

As the Empress was undergoing this transition, Victoria was also changing. Downtown was being transformed from a fairly placid dozen blocks of small stores, restaurants and tourist businesses into a busy central core surrounded by a forest of high-rise condominium towers and hotels. Civic leaders projected that eventually, some twenty thousand residents would live in the area, and encouraged the residential growth by approving high-density projects. Once a place that died at dusk, Victoria's downtown became a lively night-time destination.

In its first seventy years, the Empress Hotel had been the only first-class game in town, dominating the Inner Harbour and providing fine dining in a city where good restaurants were rare. It had long been the place for important social events and fundraisers and the destination hotel for affluent travellers. Beginning in the late 1970s, though, as tourism to the capital city increased, other hotels went up along the harbour and many more upper-end restaurants opened, a trend that accelerated in the 1990s and into the twenty-first century.

When the Empress closed for renovations in 1988, some of its traditional business drifted away to other, newer hotels. When it reopened, managers and staff set about reclaiming its place as the social centre of the city and the icon of the Inner Harbour.

"When I came to the hotel in 1991," recalls Deirdre Campbell, "my mandate was to reopen the hotel to the community. We had become the dowdy old dowager, and people had found new places to meet while we were closed; we had to find new ways to woo them back. We had to reassert the Empress as the heart and soul of this community."

The Empress came alive again with a verve that definitely took it out of the dumpy dowager class. In one annual event, teams were invited to compete in martini-making. In another, players took part in a croquet tournament on the hotel's venerable lawn. Dressed in white and swinging a mean mallet, participants roqueted and triple peeled, then partook of strawberries and cream, in support of various charities. The tournament continued for some seven or eight years, most often linked to the Pacific Opera Society. And an annual Pacific Northwest wine festival attracted winemakers and oenophiles.

In 1994, the Empress became the host hotel for the Commonwealth Games. As some 2,700 athletes, plus members of the press, officials, and thousands of spectators descended on the city for ten days in August, the Palm Court was converted to an accreditation centre for the media while the Conference Centre housed the bulk of press facilities. Dignitaries hosted events in the Crystal Ballroom; official and volunteer accreditation took place in downstairs rooms. Queen Elizabeth was the guest of honour at a lunch at the Empress; Prince Edward joined British athletes for a party in the Crystal Ballroom.

*An annual croquet tournament attracted fiercely competitive teams to the Empress lawn in the 1990s.*
THE FAIRMONT EMPRESS

The Empress catered outside events such as a downtown dinner where Prince Edward was the guest of honour. Campbell thought she had covered all bases—until the prince asked for tea. To her horror, there was not a teabag to be had. "I had to go to McDonalds to get the prince a cup of tea," she confesses sheepishly.

The restoration of the Empress as the social and fundraising centre of Victoria accelerated when John Williams, CP Hotels executive vice-president, arrived to manage the hotel in 1995. Williams deeply valued the traditions and the continuity the Empress provided, both in his own life and in the life of Victoria. His first job as an immigrant to Canada in 1967 was as a junior manager at the hotel; twenty-eight years later, he returned as manager. "The Empress has always been the social and business centre of Victoria," he says, "where Victorians celebrated King George VI's coronation, the ending of World Wars I and II, and Canada's centenary, and where Pierre Trudeau made an inspiring speech in his first leadership campaign. Her Majesty Queen Elizabeth II has visited the hotel a number of times, and every single Canadian Prime Minister and British Columbia premier since 1908 has spent time at the Empress." Williams wanted the Empress to regain its position as the city's social and community centre. Visions, the major fundraiser for the Victoria Hospitals Foundation that garners some $300,000 annually, had for several years been held elsewhere. In 1997, it returned to the Empress for its gala reception, dinner and dancing. The hotel continues as a platinum-level sponsor for the event.

From 1992 on, organizations and commercial sponsors bought and decorated Christmas trees that were then put on show for the public. In the early years, the trees were all

*Every year thousands gather on the lawns surrounding the Inner Harbour for Symphony Splash, with musicians playing from a barge moored in the harbour. One of the prime viewing points is the Fairmont Empress flag deck.*
ROB D'ESTRUBE

*The Bengal Room was recast and redecorated in 1997.*

THE FAIRMONT EMPRESS/TONY OWEN

decked out in one room then moved to various locations in the hotel. As the number of trees increased, each tree was decorated in place in the main-floor hallways of the Empress between the Conference Centre and the upper lobby. Passersby vote on their favourite trees, enclosing a donation for the British Columbia Children's Hospital with their vote; ten thousand people now see the seventy trees each year.

The Empress hosts other fundraisers such as Souper Bowls of Hope, where people buy soup from the Empress kitchen in bowls that local potters have donated, the proceeds going to help street youth.

No one will soon forget the 1997 symphony fundraiser organized by retired realtor Eric Charman, who has masterminded many such events at the Empress. "At the end of a mini performance by the symphony, I suddenly struck up Handel's fireworks music. What I had not told management was that I had secretly installed indoor fireworks in all the flower arrangements." The pyrotechnics flashed and soared, and the room filled with smoke. Charman was wearing a new and very expensive suit; flying sparks ate holes in the lapels as people crowded for the exit doors. The explosive event raised more than $200,000 for the symphony.

"Victoria is lucky to have a building of the stature of the Empress," Charman notes. "It's something you can't find in many cities, and I really appreciate it more and more, its atmosphere, its character, its charm."

The Royal Renovation of 1988–89 might have been expected to see the hotel comfortably through to its hundredth birthday in 2008. But changing travel patterns, a changing customer base and normal wear and tear resulted in a continuing series of changes and renovations from 1995 on.

The public areas of the Empress, for example, are always under stress: visitors walk through the historic hotel, thousands attend the many events at the hotel, thousands more come for afternoon tea, and locals and tourists visit the Empress Room and the Bengal Room throughout the year. The constant activity means that the Empress experiences more wear and tear than most other hotels. Hallways and function rooms all need renewal, usually every five years, with new furniture, fresh paint, new lighting, new wall coverings and new carpets.

In 1989, the Palm Court was restored to its original splendour, with the stained glass dome once more filtering softly coloured light into the room. But ten years later, it was sagging on its supports and in need of a further restoration. Victoria stained glass experts Ed Schaeffer and Tom Mercer rebuilt the dome.

The floor of the Palm Court, inlaid with tiny tiles, was also suffering. In the 1990s, in conjunction with an exhibit at the Royal British Columbia Museum across the road, Victoria sculptor Maarten Schaddelee created a one-tonne chocolate sculpture in the Palm Court—but when the time came to move it out, the weight of the sculpture cracked many of the tiles. They were removed, and interior designer Deborah Lloyd Forrest created a new floor design to be cut in marble. Seven types of marble were imported from Spain, Italy and Mexico, in shades of green, white-veined grey, gold salmon and light pink; the green marble was the last of its kind in the world. The fountain was removed from the centre of the room, "breathing life and space into another magnificent architectural jewel," notes former manager John Williams.

In 1997, the bar in the centre of the Bengal Room was moved back to the side—where it had been years earlier—and the room refurbished to look more like a gentleman's club, with leather-clad furniture and a view from all areas of the famed tiger skin. Lennie Lim witnessed this change, as he has every Bengal Room change since 1974. Born and raised in Victoria, he started work at the Empress in 1970 as a janitor, then dishwasher, then porter, before becoming a Bengal bartender. He remembers the dark, gloomy room of the 1970s and the old tiger skin, and the rattan chairs and new, smaller, and decidedly less ratty tiger skin that adorned the lounge after the 1988–89 renovations.

He explains why he stays: "It's a fun place to be, and you meet a lot of interesting people. It has an international character. And I value history: my grandfather came to Victoria in 1881; he worked for the railway and raised thirteen kids. This place is full of history. It's part of the tradition of Victoria."

In 1997, the tea lobby floor, still the original wood laid down in 1908, was refinished, the furnishings replaced and the door to the outside closed during tea times, to make the space more private. By 2007, the wood floor had worn so thin in places that a further refinishing was impossible. Plans called for the floor to be taken up and replaced for the hotel's hundredth anniversary, with the wood refashioned into mementoes of years past.

Guest rooms also needed regular renewal. In 1994–95, rooms in the centre section were renovated; in 1995–96 and again in 2000, the rooms in the Humboldt wing and the main building were refurbished.

By 1997, the storerooms were full of bolts of leftover fabric, used furniture, stately chandeliers and other items no longer in use. So the Empress did what every householder does: they held a garage sale. "The crowd started growing at about 7 A.M.," reported the *Times Colonist*, "at one point extending all the way from the ballroom through the Conference Centre entrance and halfway down the block to Humboldt Street. They waited patiently, eager to decorate their homes in early Empress.

"People examined carpets, checked out couches, looked at lampshades. Crowds thronged around tables displaying water jugs, trays, shelves from old refrigerators, money pouches and a huge Canadian flag." The sale raised some $16,000, with half going to the Victoria Women's Transition House.

The steep slopes of the Empress are roofed with heavy slate bounded by copper flashings. Over the years, slates that crashed to the ground in heavy wind were replaced and repairs done as needed, but, eighty years after the hotel opened, much of the roof was still the original. Even stone does not last forever, though, and, in 1989, roofers began the specialized task of replacing the roof, slate by slate.

"It's a never-ending job," notes chief engineer Andrew Leslie, a task undertaken by the only Victoria company that does such work, Grist Slate and Tile Roofing; the company also repairs the roof of the Legislative Buildings. Craftsmen David and Korby Grist are, section by section, removing the old slates from the steeply sloped roof and replacing them with new slates from Quebec. The copper flashing is also being replaced, this time formed around plastic piping that ensures greater durability.

The Empress needed, too, to keep up with the technological times. By 1996, advertisements for CP Hotels promised computer modem and fax hook-ups and complimentary printers for guests. A decade later, the Fairmont Empress offered a multifunction business centre and high-speed Internet connections.

Change came also deep in the bowels of the building. In 2003, a volunteer employee green team did a waste audit of what went into the garbage at the Empress. By 2007, all newspaper, cardboard, tins and plastic bottles were being recycled, and most food waste was being diverted and recycled, reducing the trash sent to landfills by more than 35 per cent. New and highly efficient grease traps in the hotel's basement collected waste grease, while above stairs, compact fluorescent bulbs rather than energy-wasting incandescent bulbs lit rooms and public spaces—though bulbs for chandeliers still posed a problem. The hotel converted its heating systems from oil to natural gas, a cleaner-burning fuel.

Changes to the building also altered the gardens and grounds, as the hotel's greenhouses were removed and a number of flower beds eliminated during the Royal Renovation to make room for the Conference Centre and the lobby addition. The Conservatory became the walkway between the Conference Centre and the hotel. Bulldozers necessarily trundled across some of the site, and, in the next few years, a number of the largest trees, including several old copper beeches and maples, succumbed to root damage. Since then, Stig Karlsson, gardener from 1967 to 1970 and head gardener from 1974 to the present, and his crew of two year-round and one seasonal gardener have been planting new trees, including beeches, maples and two weeping sequoias that frame the front path to the Empress.

Karlsson is proudly possessive of the gardens, infamous for his quick temper when someone tears up the grass or damages the flowers, and intent on providing the best possible show for guests and Victorians. He counts himself lucky to do the job he does. "Gardening is therapy to a lot of people. I'm in therapy all the time. I love what I do. It just mellows me out."

*Craft roofer Korby Grist replaces slates on the hotel's sharply sloping roof.*
THE FAIRMONT EMPRESS/
TONY OWEN

His first passion is the Empress roses, some thirty varieties in twenty-five beds on the south side of the hotel. In every colour of the rose rainbow, some perfumed, all free-blooming from the end of April until the middle of November, the Empress roses are the mainstay of the gardens. Also featured are some 18,000 bulbs, mostly tulips, that brighten the beds from March through May, summer geraniums in four colours and other summer- and fall-blooming annuals.

For the hotel's hundredth anniversary in 2008, Karlsson and the other gardeners are converting a former dry pond area at the northwest corner of the property into a centennial garden, with lawns, flowers, a fountain and a seating area.

The twenty-first century brought a major shift in the core business at the Fairmont Empress. In the 1990s, a high percentage of the hotel's guests arrived on tours from Japan, the United States, Canada, Korea and Britain. When bus tours filled the rooms, no hotel restaurant could feed the large tours quickly, efficiently and to the standards of the Empress. The Garden Cafe, long a downstairs feature, was closed, to reopen in 1997 as Kiplings, a dining room featuring hot, cold and dessert buffets. Its sumptuous array quickly became popular with Victorians, especially in the off-season. The seafood line-up regularly included trays of prawns, crab legs, oysters and salmon three ways: smoked, candied and marinated. The dinner buffet included a carvery, with beef, ham and turkey. There were few who could resist a second and even third trip to the dessert table, with its signature bread and butter and baked rice puddings, as well as more decadent desserts such as cheesecakes, flans and crème brûlée.

By 2005, while the number of independent travellers grew, the bus tour business had all but evaporated. Kiplings closed, and the Empress Room, encompassing the Lobby Lounge overlooking the harbour, opened for three meals a day.

Roger Soane worked at the Empress as food and beverage manager, then as operations manager, in the 1990s. When he returned as general manager in 2005 from assignments in other Fairmont hotels, he accomplished something he had long dreamed of: he opened the verandah that runs along the harbour side of the hotel outside the tea lobby windows, from May through September—or as long as the weather co-operates. Available at first for drinks and appetizers, it soon became a favourite for lunch and dinner.

When the Empress opened in 1908, European cuisine and imported foods were the hallmarks of a fine dining room. Ninety years later, West Coast chefs were apt to look closer to home for their ingredients and recipes. Speaking of executive sous-chef Candace Penrose, a *Globe and Mail* writer noted in 1994 that, "All season long, she haunts the backroads of the Saanich Peninsula to gather ingredients from supersweet crunchy corn to Bear Hill Orchards apple juice, the best I have tasted anywhere in Canada. When gooseberry chutney appears beside the pan-roasted Arctic char, or wild blackberry ginger butter complements the baked B.C. salmon filet, they are from Candy's pantry." That trend accelerated through the 1990s and into the hotel's tenth decade.

As its core business shifted to independent travellers, the Empress recognized the need to pamper its individual guests. In 1996, the hotel introduced Entrée Gold—later renamed Fairmont Gold—a "hotel within a hotel" for guests prepared to pay a little extra. Gold

*Stig Karlsson cares for his prized roses in the Empress rose gardens.*
THE FAIRMONT EMPRESS/
TONY OWEN

*The verandah on the front of the hotel has become a favourite place for Victorians and visitors to sample a glass of wine or have a meal.*
THE FAIRMONT EMPRESS/
TONY OWEN

guests were guaranteed either a harbour view or a large room in the separate section of the hotel. They had use of a Gold lounge with an honour bar, complimentary breakfast and a Gold concierge, and enjoyed separate check-in and personalized service.

The rooms on the eighth floor of the hotel, which had awkward sloped ceilings and lacked private bathrooms, had been used for staff accommodation. In 2000, hotel managers decided to take advantage of their superb views and unusual architecture by combining eight rooms and some other spaces to create four new eclectic and original guest rooms under the dormers.

The Empress also built a spa: where locals once got down and dirty in the Beaver Pub, guests could now get relaxed and clean in the Willow Stream Spa, opened in 2002 under the aegis of a separate company that operated spas in nine Fairmont hotels. The $6 million, 740-square-metre centre contained eleven treatment rooms, a mineral soaking pool, and a waterfall at the entrance. The top-of-the-line spa experience, with everything from a body polish to a traditional European facial, lasted seven hours.

The Royal Renovation prompted changes in the hotel retail shops. Rick Arora, who owns all but one of those stores, recalls that, prior to 1989, they sold much the same merchandise as could be found in any souvenir shop on Government Street. "The most expensive piece in the shops was $39." But, after 1989, they went increasingly high-end, with pieces costing up to $150,000 in the art gallery and leather and fur shops. When one of the richest men in Asia dropped by the art gallery some years ago, he spent $200,000; on his next visit, his purchases totalled $430,000.

"We tried to give people something different, something they couldn't get anywhere else in Victoria," says Arora of the Canadian art, custom-made jewellery and Italian-designed leather and furs.

At the same time, ever dependent on air and ferry transportation to bring customers to Vancouver Island, the Empress looked for partners such as the Victoria *Clipper*, the catamaran fast-ferry service that linked Victoria and Seattle. The *Clipper* and the Empress combined to offer ferry, accommodation, spa and dining packages for island visitors.

Although change was a constant at the hotel, the emphasis on excellence in guest service remained the same. Guest service co-ordinator Deborah Sleno exemplifies the philosophy of superb service: in 2001 she won the Fairmont-wide employee of the year award. She knew from the moment she took a part-time job at another Victoria hotel while she was in high school that the Empress was the place for her. "I thought to myself, if I am going to work in this industry, I should work at the best place in Victoria. I came here every second day until they hired me."

Eighteen years old in 1983, she recalls that she knew it was an important job she was doing as an ambassador to people from all over the world. She's been at the hotel ever since, moving from cleaning sixteen rooms a day to working on the front desk to being tour co-ordinator to her present position as lobby concierge and guest agent. Although her first job in housekeeping meant hard work—"It was pretty rigorous—when you went home at the end of the day, you were basically spent"—the job of concierge presented more unusual challenges.

Many requests she has received from guests are routine—flowers for a wife's birthday, parcels to be couriered, guest itineraries to arrange—but others required more thought. She has been asked where and how to buy a Jersey cow, a totem pole and a penny farthing, although not all for the same person.

Title of the longest-serving employee at the Empress belongs to Lawrie Harrison, an in-room dining attendant, who came to the hotel in September of 1966. "When I got my driver's licence, my mother would tell me to give my granny a ride; she's going to the Empress for an old age pensioners' meeting. Well, I'd give her a ride up to the old entrance, and I'd be looking up and thinking, 'Wow! She's going to that huge building!' And I decided I'd try to get a job here."

He has seen naked people, including an eighty-year-old woman, open the door when he arrives with their meals. He has served George C. Scott—who invited him to sit down and have a beer—and Bob Hope, who came to the door in his underwear and liked a breakfast that included boiled eggs and warm prunes. He has served other stars, politicians and thousands of ordinary people. His rewards come from the people he meets. "And 99.9 per cent of them are nice."

Guests rarely see the kitchen workers and chefs, but they and the other behind-the-scenes employees are crucial to the hotel's success. Soso Wong, *chef de partie* in charge of the cold kitchen station, has been working at the Empress for almost thirty-five years. Born in China, she came to Victoria as a baby with her family and continued the family tradition of hard work. Wanting a job somewhere other than her family's dim sum restaurant, she chose the Empress while still in high school and never left, working at the hotel part-time through her studies in hotel management and continuing full time after graduation.

She started as a pantry girl, setting up four hundred afternoon tea trays every day, helping to prepare food for as many as a thousand people a day. She still remembers how to make the honey crumpets then a feature of tea time—toast once, spread with honey butter, let cool a little, then toast again—but now she is in charge of cold food preparation for buffets and other events as well as afternoon tea.

She echoes what other long-time employees have said: "This is my second home. The people here are like brothers and sisters to me."

In 2008, the Empress heads into its second century. More change is on the way. In the next several years, the bus station that has stood on Empress property at the corner of Douglas and Belleville for many decades will be moved some ten blocks north, and the corner will be used for other development. The Crystal Garden, the venerable glass-roofed building originally built as a recreation centre and swimming pool, survived troubled times, and the City of Victoria is taking it over as an adjunct to the Conference Centre.

But the Empress experience will remain founded on the hotel's iconic existence as the

*Long-time employees Soso
Wong, Lennie Lim
and Joga (Yogi) Kaler represent
among them almost
a hundred years of service
at the Empress.*
THE FAIRMONT EMPRESS/

TONY OWEN

centrepiece of the city's Inner Harbour and on its philosophy of service. In 2001, *Globe and Mail* editor Victor Dwyer visited Victoria and showed up for tea at the Empress without a reservation. He expected the worst; he got the best. He was amazed. "And that's when it hit me," he wrote, "the reason for my semi-flustered bafflement. It was simple, really: I was paying money for service in our much-vaunted service economy—and I was getting it. Here, in the rarefied atmosphere of the Empress Tea Room, surrounded by brocade curtains and antique chandeliers and dour portraits of long-dead royals, I was... being served. And I was so unused to good service that I had felt suspicion, then confusion, and now, simply, a bit of heady nirvana."

That feeling seems set to endure as the Grand Old Lady of Government Street takes on her second century.

# BIBLIOGRAPHY

BARRETT, ANTHONY, AND RHODRI LISCOMBE. *Francis Rattenbury and British Columbia.* Vancouer: University of British Columbia Press, 1983.

CAMPBELL, ROBERT A. *Demon Rum or Easy Money: Government Control of Liquor in British Columbia from Prohibition to Privatization.* Ottawa: Carleton University Press, 1991.

CARR, EMILY. *The Emily Carr Omnibus.* Vancouver/Toronto: Douglas & McIntyre, 1993.

CASH, GWEN. *I Like British Columbia.* Toronto: Macmillan of Canada, 1939.

CASH, GWEN. *A Million Miles from Ottawa.* Toronto: Macmillan of Canada, 1942.

CASH, GWEN. *Off the Record. The Personal Reminiscences of Canada's First Woman Reporter.* Langley, B.C.: Stagecoach, 1977.

CASH, GWEN. Scrapbooks. Uncatalogued. British Columbia Archives and Records Service.

CRAWFORD, L.B., AND J.G. SUTHERLAND. "The Empress of Victoria. Sixty-five Years of Foundation Settlements," Canadian Geotechnical Journal, vol. 8, 1971.

GIBSON, GORDON, AND CAROL RENISON. *Bull of the Woods. The Gordon Gibson Story.* Vancouver/Toronto: Douglas & McIntyre, 1980.

HOLLOWAY, GODFREY. *The Empress of Victoria.* Victoria: Pacifica, 1968.

HUTCHISON, BRUCE. "The Eccentric Empress of Victoria" in *Maclean's,* 15 December 1950.

KEITH, AGNES NEWTON. *Three Came Home.* Boston: Atlantic Monthly-Little Brown, 1947.

KIPLING, RUDYARD. *Letters of Travel (1892–1913).* London: Macmillan, 1920.

MCKELWAY, ST. CLAIR. *True Tales from the Annals of Crime and Rascality.* New York: Random House, 1951.

REKSTEN, TERRY. *"More English Than the English." A Very Social History of Victoria.* Victoria: Orca, 1986.

REKSTEN, TERRY. *Rattenbury.* Victoria: Sono Nis Press, 1978.

Report submitted by the CPR Departments of Hotel, Engineering, and Real Estate regarding the Empress Hotel, 1965. Canadian Pacific Archives.

SHAUGHNESSY, ALFRED. *Both Ends of the Candle.* Toronto: Lester and Orpen, 1978.

STURSBERG, PETER. *Those Where the Days.* Toronto: Peter Martin, 1969.

TURNER, ROBERT D. *The Pacific Empresses.* Victoria: Sono Nis Press, 1981.

TURNER, ROBERT D. *The Pacific Princesses.* Victoria: Sono Nis Press, 1977.

Other sources include interviews (see Preface), and clipping files and miscellaneous papers (reports, correspondence, brochures, hotel bills, menus, pamphlets and signage) held by the Empress Hotel Archives, the Canadian Pacific Archives, the Victoria City Archives and the British Columbia Archives and Records Service.

# INDEX